The Gospel According To John 1-10 (Volume 1)

A unique verse-by-verse study of the Bible

Psalm 1:1-3: Blessed is the man that walketh not in the counsel of the ungodly, nor standeth in the way of sinners, nor sitteth in the seat of the scornful. But his delight is in the law of the LORD; and in his law doth he meditate day and night. And he shall be like a tree planted by the rivers of water, that bringeth forth his fruit in his season; his leaf also shall not wither; and whatsoever he doeth shall prosper.

Rev. James Bussard, B.B.S., M.Min.

All Scripture quotations are from the *Authorized (King James) Version of the Bible.*

All definitions, footnotes, and commentaries came from the following three sources:

      1. Strong's Exhaustive Concordance of the Bible

      2. Thayer's Greek Lexicon

      3. Webster's 1828 Dictionary

The definitions, footnotes, and commentaries provided are given as accurately as possible and are based upon the sources listed above. These studies do in no way proclaim themselves to be without error, even though the utmost care was taken to be accurate and faithful to the Word of God.

These studies were developed for a person using the *Authorized (King James) Version of the Bible.* A person that uses these studies with other versions may not be able to use them as efficiently.

Preface

I am the pastor of a small church in Mid-Maryland and have a young family. My wife and I regularly work with our children (especially with our oldest daughter, who is nine) to develop the habit of reading their Bibles every day. I preach and teach to our church family that we are given God's Word for a reason. It is only through regular study that we show ourselves approved unto God (*II Timothy 2:15*). It is only through faithful application of what we learn that our lives are successful in God's sight (*Joshua 1:8*). The Bible claims to be the only divine book on Earth that was given to us by God (*II Timothy 3:16*) to explain who He is, who we are, what are purpose is, who His Son, Jesus Christ, is, and much, much more. However, what good is the Bible to a person that does not know how to study it? What good is it to someone that does not know how to apply what they have learned? Generally, many believers get frustrated with churches, pastors, and the Bible in particular, because of these very occurrences. My daughter was not exempt.

My daughter, who has a heart for God and wants to know Him, was not getting anything out of her Bible reading. For instance, she would read in the *Psalms* and come up with, "God wants me to witness more," as an application. Now, that application is fine when offered up one time, but not when offered after reading every psalm! It was at that point the Holy Spirit revealed to me that she did not understand what she was reading and that I needed to do something about it; not just as a pastor, but as a father!

As a result, I began to look for studies that would help her understand her reading. After looking through the primary venues available to the average, American believer, I realized that there was nothing for her. Most Bible studies feed the individual what the teacher wants them to learn. Others do not encourage study or application of the scriptures. After a time, God impressed upon my heart to begin work on something that would allow a person to study the scriptures without frustration and know exactly what the Bible is talking about through any given chapter, which is the product you have before you. The purpose of these studies is fourfold:

1. To emphasize the need of Bible reading, study, and application in the Christian life

Many believers do not pick up their Bibles and/or are not encouraged to. It is a pastor's duty to take God's Word and explain it through preaching and teaching, especially to his congregation. These studies are set up so that a person can take a chapter (or portion of one) and study it day by day. This way the reader has a way to track their own progress through the Word of God, which is an encouragement in itself.

2. To explain the sometimes hard to understand language of the King James Version

I preach and teach from the King James Version of the scriptures and encourage our people to do the same. I have my reasons for doing so, which are not important to the purpose of these Bible studies. Though this translation is used exclusively in my preaching, I will be the first to admit that the language can be difficult to understand and define. The English Bible was translated from Hebrew and Greek, which not many people have studied today. However, many resources exist to help our study. It is my desire to take the language of the King James Version and define it, when needed, through those existing tools. This essentially takes out the middle-man and faithfully puts the foreign languages into modern English. Though I may commentate a little, the intent is not to make this into a commentary.

3. To encourage Christians to think about what God is saying to us through the scriptures

It is a pastor's duty to teach his congregation to have a personal relationship with God for themselves. This is very rare in many congregations. We either have lazy Christians that will not study or lazy, prideful pastors that want to control their congregations. God wants to know the individual believer personally; not through their pastor. The Lord desires that all believers be thinking people. The only way to have a thinking person is to ask them questions. These Bible studies are setup to inspire the believer to consider the scriptures through simple questions and fill-in-the blanks. It does not have an agenda behind it other than this. It simply walks through the Bible and explains it.

4. To expose the believer to a growing relationship with God through the reading of the scriptures

Few believers have a relationship with God today. Their lack of Bible reading is part of that problem. If we read the scriptures every day, we will learn about God and how to be more like Him. If we apply the scriptures to our lives, we will grow closer to our Creator. These studies are but tools to help the average believer read their Bible and know their God better. This is applicable for every age and profitable for growth.

If God helps you to grow in your relationship with Him through these lessons, I hope you will share it with me (*HeritageParkPastor@Gmail.com*). Thank you for your interest in the scriptures. May God bless you as you walk with the Lord Jesus and learn of Him in His Word.

Best Regards,

Rev. James Bussard, B.B.S., M.Min.
Pastor of Heritage Park Baptist Church, Keymar, MD

Bible Study Questions (*John 1:1-51*)

Instructions: Pray that God will help you to understand this passage. Read through this Bible passage twice: once for reading and another time for understanding. After reading, consider and answer the questions listed below. Write down notes regarding anything else God spoke to you about.

1. Who existed in the beginning (*the beginning of all things*) (*v.1*)[1]?

   _____ (GOD) + the WORD _____

2. What things are true regarding the Word (*v.1-2*)?

   a. He was with __GOD_____

   b. He was ____GOD_____

   c. He was in the __beginning_____ with ____GOD_____ (*v.2*)

3. What important action did the Word perform (*v.3*)?

   _____ ALL THINGS WERE MADE BY HIM _____

4. Was there any part of Creation that the Word did not make (*v.3*)?

   _____ NO _____

5. Does this mean that He created you (*Psalm 139:14*)?

   _____ YES _____

6. What existed in the Word (*v.4*)[2]?

   __ LIFE   (LIGHT) _____

7. What was this in regards to men (*v.4*)[3]?

   __ LIFE WAS THE LIGHT OF MEN _____

8. What did the light do (*v.5*)[4]?

   _____ SHINES IN THE DARKNESS _____

9. What did the darkness do in return (*v.5*)[5]? → COMPREHEND

   __ DID NOT OVERCOME THE LIGHT = REJECTED IT __

10. Who was sent from God (*v.6*)[6]?

    __ A MAN CALLED JOHN _____

---

[1] ***John 1:1***: The Word is *another name for Jesus Christ*

[2] ***John 1:4***: This life speaks of *the fullness of life, both essential and ethical, which belongs to God and Christ alone*

[3] ***John 1:4b***: This life being the light of men means *God transfused life into His creation which in turn became Man's intelligence and self-consciousness*

[4] ***John 1:5***: Light and darkness are used metaphorically regarding Truth being brought to those ignorant of it

[5] ***John 1:5b***: To comprehend means *to take for one's self* (in this case: regarding the world rejecting divine Truth)

[6] ***John 1:6***: This John was not the author (John the apostle), but John the Baptist

11. Why was John sent by God (**v.7**)?

     a. To _WITNESS_____ (*to come with divine authority*) for a _____

     (*regarding the testimony establishing the Messiahship and divinity of Jesus*)

     b. To bear _____ (*to give testimony*) of the _____

12. Why did John bear witness that Jesus was the Messiah (**v.7**)?

_____

13. Was John the Baptist the Light (*the Messiah*) (**v.8**)?

_____

14. What then was John the Baptist's duty (**v.8**)?

_____

15. Besides God sending him, why else did John the Baptist bear witness of the Light (**v.9**)?

     a. Because He was the _____ Light (*the true Messiah*)

     b. Because the Light _____ (*to give divine knowledge to*) every man that

     _____ into the world

16. What else was true regarding the Light (**v.10-11**)?

     a. He was _____ the world (*the human race*)

     b. The world was _____ (*to come into existence*) by Him

     c. The world _____ Him not (*to know His divinity*)

     d. He _____ unto His own (*His own land, city, temple, Messianic rights,*

     and possessions) (**v.11**)

     e. His own (*His own people*) _____ Him not (*to not acknowledge who*

     He professed to be)

17. What happened to those that did receive Him (**v.12**)[7]?

_____

18. What are the qualifications for becoming a son of God (**v.12**)?

     a. _____ Jesus Christ (*to accept His claim as the Messiah and Creator*)

     b. _____ (*to commit oneself trustfully to*) on the name of Jesus Christ

---

[7] **John 1:12**: To be given power to become sons of God means *to be given the ability to become sons of God*

19. What is true about the spiritual birth of those that became the sons of God (*v.13*)[8]?

      a. They were not born of _____ (*human descent or generation*)

      b. They were not born of the will (*desire*) of the _____ (*sexual desire*)

      c. They were not born of the will of _____

      d. They were born of _____

20. What else was true about the Word (*v.14*)[9]?

      a. He was made _____ (*to enter into participation of human nature*)

      b. He _____ (*to live*) among us

      c. We _____ (*to look upon*) His _____ (*the personal excellence of Christ, in which He excels by virtue of His nature*)

      d. He was full of _____ and _____ (*the absolute Truth of God's Word*)

21. When the world beheld Jesus' glory, what did they see in Him (*v.14*)?

_____

22. What was John the Baptist's witness (*to testify*) of the Word made flesh (*v.15*)?

      a. "This was He of whom I _____..."

      b. "He that _____ after me is _____ (*to come into existence*) before me: for He was _____ (*to be first in succession*) me..."

23. What do all those that believe in Jesus Christ receive (*v.16*)[10]?

      a. His _____

      b. _____ for _____ (*the gift of grace offered to all believers: salvation*)

24. What man gave the Law to Israel from God (*v.17*)?

_____

25. What came by Jesus Christ (*v.17*)?

_____

---

[8] *John 1:13*: Speaking of *God birthing us into His family, when we believe in Jesus Christ, to become His children in reality and not just right and privilege*

[9] *John 1:14*: The grace exhibited by Jesus Christ speaks of *His pity for sinful men that moved Him to leave His position in Heaven and voluntarily undergo the hardships and miseries of the human life, and by His sufferings and death procure salvation for mankind*

[10] *John 1:16*: Of His fullness refers to *John 1:14* where Jesus is said to be full of grace and truth; all believers partake of this fullness

26. Who has seen God at any time (**v.18**)?

_____

27. Who has declared (*to unfold*) the things about God (**v.18**)?

_____

28. In what special place is the Son that He can accurately declare things about the Father (**v.18**)[11]?

_____

29. Whose record (*testimony*) is John about to present (**v.19**)[12]?

_____

30. Who came to question this man (**v.19**)?

    a. The _____ (*one who offers sacrifices and performs sacred rites*)

    b. The _____ (*assistants to the priests*)

31. What did they ask John the Baptist (**v.19**)?

_____

32. What did John confess (*to declare*) before them (**v.20**)?

_____

33. What other questions did these men ask John the Baptist (**v.21**)?

    a. "Are you _____ (*Elijah*)?"

    b. "Are you that _____ (*a prophet that would come just before*

    the Messiah established His Kingdom on Earth*)?"

34. What was John's answer to each of these questions (**v.21**)?

_____

35. What were their next questions for John the Baptist (**v.22**)?

    a. "_____ are you?"

    b. "What do you have to _____ of yourself?"

36. Why were they asking these questions (**v.22**)?

_____

37. What was John's answer (**v.23**)?

_____

38. What was the one crying in the wilderness to say (**v.23**)?

_____

---

[11] **John 1:18**: In the bosom of the Father means *in the closest and most intimate relation to the Father*

[12] **John 1:19**: This is John the Baptist

39. What prophet made this prophecy in the Old Testament (**v.23**)[13]?

_____

40. What group had sent these men to question John the Baptist (**v.24**)?

_____

41. What did these men question John about next, since he did not claim to be the Messiah, that

prophet, or Elijah (**v.25**)[14]? _____

42. What did John state that he baptized (*to immerse*) with (**v.26**)?

_____

43. What did he have to say about a certain person (**v.26-27**)?

    a. He _____ among (*to live in the midst of*) them

    b. They _____ Him not

    c. He would come _____ John, but was preferred (*to come into existence*)

    _____ him (*denoting higher rank*) (**v.27**)

    d. John was not worthy to _____ His shoe's latchet (*a sandal strap*)

44. Where were these things done (**v.28**)?

_____

45. What was John doing there (**v.28**)?

_____

46. Who did John the Baptist see the next day (**v.29**)?

_____

47. What did he tell those around him (**v.29**)?

_____

48. What work did John say Jesus would do (**v.29**)?

_____

49. Did Jesus come to teach before or after John the Baptist (**v.30**)?

_____

50. Was Jesus preferred (*to come into existence*) before or after John (**v.30**)?

_____

51. Did Jesus exist before or after John the Baptist (**v.30**)?

_____

_____

[13] **John 1:23**: cross-reference: **Isaiah 40:3**

[14] **John 1:25**: To baptize means *to immerse or submerge* (in this case: into water)

52. What else did John say about Jesus (**v.31**)?

    a. "I _____ (*to personally know*) Him not..."

    b. "I knew that He should be made _____ (*to become known*) to Israel..."

    c. "Because of this, I come _____ (*to immerse*) with water."

53. What did John bare record (*to bear testimony*) of (**v.32**)?

    a. He saw the _____ descending from Heaven like a _____

    b. The _____ abode on (*to put forth constant influence*) Him

54. Did John know Jesus personally before God revealed Him to be the Messiah (**v.33**)?

_____

55. Who told John how to identify the Messiah (**v.33**)?

_____

56. How would John identify the Messiah (**v.33**)?

    a. He would see the Spirit _____ (*to come down*)

    b. He would see the Spirit _____ with Him

57. What special work would the Messiah perform (**v.33**)[15]?

_____

58. When John saw this occur to Jesus, what was his testimony (**v.34**)?

_____

59. Who was standing with John the next day (**v.35**)[16]?

_____

60. When John saw Jesus, what did he say (**v.36**)[17]?

_____

61. What did John's two disciples do when they heard him say that (**v.37**)[18]?

_____

62. What did Jesus do when He saw them following Him (**v.38**)?

    a. He _____

    b. He said, "What do you _____?"

---

[15] **John 1:33**: To baptize one in the Holy Ghost means *to immerse one into the Spirit of God* (speaking of salvation)
[16] **John 1:35**: A disciple is *a learner or pupil*
[17] **John 1:36**: The Lamb of God refers to *Jesus being likened to a sacrificial lamb on account of His death, innocently and patiently endured, to atone for sin*
[18] **John 1:37**: To follow means *to join one as an attendant and accompany him*

63. What was their answer (**v.38**)[19]?

_____

64. What is another word for *Rabbi* (**v.38**)[20]?

_____

65. How did Jesus reply (**v.39**)?

_____

66. What did the two followers do in turn (**v.39**)?

        a. They _____

        b. They _____ where he dwelt

        c. They _____ with Him that day

67. About what time did this conversation take place (**v.39**)[21]?

_____

68. What was the name of one of John's former disciples (**v.40**)?

_____

69. Who was this man's brother (**v.40**)?

_____

70. After Andrew found Jesus, what was the first thing he did (**v.41**)?

_____

71. What did he say to Peter (**v.41**)?

_____

72. What is another word for *Messiah* (**v.41**)?

_____

73. What did Andrew do with Peter (**v.42**)?

_____

74. What did Jesus say when He saw Peter (**v.42**)?

        a. "You are _____ son of Jona…"

        b. "You shall be called _____…"

75. What is the interpretation of *Cephas* (**v.42**)?

_____

_____

[19] **John 1:38**: To dwell means *to lodge as a guest*
[20] **John 1:38c**: Master means *teacher*
[21] **John 1:39**: The tenth hour was about 4pm (6pm was the end of the Jewish day)

76. Where did Jesus go the next day (**v.43**)?

_____

77. Who did Jesus find while He was there (**v.43**)?

_____

78. What did Jesus say to this man (**v.43**)?

_____

79. Where did Philip live (**v.44**)?

_____

80. Who else lived in this city (**v.44**)?

_____

81. Who did Philip find, after being called by Jesus (**v.45**)?

_____

82. Who did Philip say they had found (**v.45**)[22]?

    a. Him, of whom _____ in the Law, and the _____, wrote

    b. _____ of Nazareth, the son of _____

83. What was Nathanael's reply (**v.46**)?

_____

84. How did Philip answer him (**v.46**)?

_____

85. What did Jesus say about Nathanael when He saw him (**v.47**)?

    a. He was an _____ indeed

    b. He had no _____ (*deceit*) within him

86. What was Nathanael's reply to Jesus (**v.48**)[23]?

_____

87. When did Jesus say that He saw Nathanael (**v.48**)?

    a. Before _____ called (*to summon*) him

    b. When he was under the _____ tree

88. Do you think that, if Jesus saw Nathanael, that He also sees you where you are?

_____

_____

[22] **John 1:45**: Moses and the prophets is another term for the Old Testament
[23] **John 1:48** (literal): *"How is it that you know me?"*

89. What was Nathanael's response to Jesus' prophecy (**v.49**)?

     a. "Rabbi, you are the _____ of God…"

     b. "Rabbi, you are the _____ of Israel."

90. How did Jesus answer his profession of faith (**v.50**)?

     a. "Because I said unto you, 'I saw you under the _____ tree,' do you _____?"

     b. "You shall see _____ things than these."

91. What things did Jesus tell Nathanael that he would surely see (**v.51**)[24]?

     a. _____ would open

     b. The _____ of God would ascend and descend upon the Son of Man

     (*Jesus Christ*)

---

[24] **John 1:51**: Verily mean *truly or of a truth*

Meditation (What God Spoke to Me About):

_____
_____
_____
_____
_____
_____
_____
_____

Application (How I Can Apply What I Learned):

_____
_____
_____
_____
_____
_____
_____
_____
_____

Memorization (How I Can Retain What I Read):

Suggestions: *John 1:1-5; 1:10-12; 1:14; 1:19-23; 1:36*

_____
_____
_____

Assessment (How I Am Doing With My Application and Memorization):

_____
_____
_____
_____
_____
_____

Bible Study Questions (*John 2:1-25*)

Instructions: Pray that God will help you to understand this passage. Read through this Bible passage twice: once for reading and another time for understanding. After reading, consider and answer the questions listed below. Write down notes regarding anything else God spoke to you about.

1. What happened on the third day (*v.1*)?

_____

2. Where was this event held (*v.1*)?

_____

3. Who was at the wedding (*v.1*)?

_____

4. Who else was called (*to be invited*) to the wedding (*v.2*)?

      a. _____

      b. His _____

5. What did the people of the wedding want (*to lack*) (*v.3*)?

_____

6. What did Jesus' mother say to Him (*v.3*)?

_____

7. What was Jesus' response (*v.4*)[25]?

      a. "_____, what have I to do with you?"

      b. "My _____ (*an opportune time*) is not yet come."

8. What did His mother say to the servants regarding Jesus (*v.5*)?

_____

9. What was set (*to stand*) near them (*v.6*)?

_____

10. What were these used for (*v.6*)[26]?

_____

11. How much water did these hold apiece (*v.6*)[27]?

_____

_____

---

[25] **John 2:4**: To call His mother, "Woman," was a respectful address in Jesus' time
[26] **John 2:6**: This purification is *the washings of the Jews before and after meals*
[27] **John 2:6c**: Three firkins is *about twenty gallons* (possibly more)

12. What did Jesus command the servants to do (**v.7**)?

_____

13. How full did the servants fill the pots (**v.7**)?

_____

14. What was Jesus' next command to the servants (**v.8**)[28]?

        a. "_____ out now…"

        b. "_____ (*to bring to*) unto the _____ (*the*

        table-master) of the feast."

15. What did the servants do (**v.8**)?

_____

16. Do you think it took faith in Jesus' work for the servants to take the water made wine to the

governor of the feast (**v.8**)? _____

17. What did the governor of the feast do (**v.9**)?

        a. He _____ the water made wine

        b. He did not know _____ the water made wine was from

        c. He _____ the bridegroom (*a newly married man*)

18. Who knew where the water made wine came from (**v.9**)?

_____

19. What was always put out at the beginning of the feast (**v.10**)[29]?

_____

20. What would be put out when men had well drunk (*to become drunken*) (**v.10**)?

_____

21. What did the governor think had been kept until the end of the feast (**v.10**)?

_____

22. Who was the one responsible for this miracle (**v.11**)?

_____

23. Was this the first, second or third miracle that Jesus performed (**v.11**)?

_____

---

[28] **John 2:8**: The governor of the feast had the duty of placing the couches and tables in order, arranging the courses, and tasting the food and wine beforehand

[29] **John 2:10**: Good means *superior to all others*

24. What happened when Jesus performed this miracle (**v.11**)?

     a. He _____ (*to make visible*) forth His glory

     b. His disciples _____ (*to have faith*) on Him

25. Where did Jesus go after the wedding (**v.12**)?

_____

26. Who went with Jesus (**v.12**)?

     a. His _____

     b. His _____ (*siblings*)

     c. His _____

27. How long did they stay in this place (**v.12**)?

_____

28. To what city did Jesus go next (**v.13**)?

_____

29. What special event was happening there (**v.13**)[30]?

_____

30. What did Jesus find in the temple (**v.14**)[31]?

     a. Those that _____ oxen and sheep

     b. The changers of _____

31. What did Jesus do, when He saw this (**v.15**)?

     a. He made a _____ (*a whip*) of small cords

     b. He _____ (*to cast out*) them all out of the temple

     c. He _____ (*to cast out*) out the sheep and oxen

     d. He _____ out the changers' money

     e. He _____ (*to turn upside-down*) the tables

32. What did Jesus say to those that sold doves (**v.16**)?

     a. "Take these things _____ (*from this place*)..."

     b. "Make not my Father's _____ a house of _____

     (*a place where trade occurs*)."

33. What did Jesus' disciples remember was written (**v.17**)[32]?

_____

_____

[30] **John 2:13**: This was the feast of the Passover that extended from the fourteenth to the twentieth day of the month Nisan (usually falling between March and April)

[31] **John 2:14**: The oxen and sheep were sold for sacrifices, while the money-changers made small change

34. What did the Jews look for, because of Jesus' actions (*v.18*)?

_____

35. What was Jesus' sign for them (*v.19*)?

      a. "_____ (*to demolish*) this temple..."

      b. "...In _____ days I will raise (*to construct*) this temple up."

36. How many years did the Jews spend building the temple in Jerusalem (*v.20*)?

_____

37. Did they believe that Jesus could build the temple in three days (*v.20*)?

_____

38. Was Jesus speaking of raising a building or his body (*v.21*)?

_____

39. When did Jesus' disciples remember that He had said this to them (*v.22*)?

_____

40. What happened to them when they remembered this (*v.22*)?

      a. They _____ the scripture

      b. They _____ the word which Jesus had said

41. What happened on the feast day of Passover (*v.23*)[33]?

_____

42. When did they believe in Jesus (*v.23*)?

_____

43. What did Jesus do in return (*v.24*)[34]?

_____

44. Why did He not do this (*v.24*)?

_____

45. Did Jesus need someone to testify of Man (*v.25*)?

_____

46. Why did He not need this (*v.25*)[35]?

_____

_____

[32] *John 2:17* (lit.): (cf. *Psalm 69:9*): **"My strong emotions for God's house have consumed the strength of my body and mind."**

[33] *John 2:23*: To believe means *to put faith towards*

[34] *John 2:24*: To commit means *to entrust oneself to and put faith in*

[35] *John 2:25*: Knowing what was in man means *that Jesus knew their hearts and all that they were* (since He is the Creator God)

Meditation (What God Spoke to Me About):

_____

_____

_____

_____

_____

_____

_____

Application (How I Can Apply What I Learned):

_____

_____

_____

_____

_____

_____

_____

_____

_____

_____

_____

Memorization (How I Can Retain What I Read):

Suggestions: _John 2:14-16; 2:24-25_

_____

_____

_____

Assessment (How I Am Doing With My Application and Memorization):

_____

_____

_____

_____

_____

Bible Study Questions (*John 3:1-36*)

Instructions: Pray that God will help you to understand this passage. Read through this Bible passage twice: once for reading and another time for understanding. After reading, consider and answer the questions listed below. Write down notes regarding anything else God spoke to you about.

1. Who came to see Jesus by night (**v.1**)?

     a. A man of the _____

     b. A man named _____

     c. A _____ (*a member of the Sanhedrin*) of the Jews

2. At what time did this man come to see Jesus (**v.2**)?

_____

3. What title did this man give Jesus (**v.2**)[36]?

_____

4. What did the Pharisees have to say about Jesus (**v.2**)?

_____

5. Why did they believe this (**v.2**)?

_____

6. What was Jesus' truthful answer to Nicodemus' praise (**v.3**)[37]?

_____

7. To be clear, what must happen for a person to enter God's kingdom (**v.3**)?

_____

8. What was Nicodemus' response to Jesus (**v.4**)?

     a. "How can a man be _____ when he is old?"

     b. "Can he _____ a second time into his mother's womb and be

     _____?"

9. Did Nicodemus understand what Jesus was really talking about?

_____

10. What did Jesus explain we have to be born of in order to enter into His kingdom (**v.5**)?

     a. We must be born of _____ (*speaking of physical birth*)

     b. We must be born of _____ (*speaking of spiritual birth*)

---

[36] **John 3:2**: Rabbi was *an honorific title for a teacher*
[37] **John 3:3**: To be born again means *to be born over again or born anew*

11. What does a person of the flesh (*natural man*) give birth to (*v.6*)[38]?

_____

12. What does the Spirit of God give birth to (*v.6*)?

_____

13. What statement did Jesus tell Nicodemus not to marvel (*to wonder*) about (*v.7*)?

_____

14. What things are true about the wind (*v.8*)?

     a. It blows where it _____ (*to desire*)

     b. We can hear the _____ of it

     c. We cannot tell where it _____ or where it _____

15. Who operates like the wind to help men become born again (*v.8*)?

_____

16. What was Nicodemus' response to Jesus' teaching (*v.9*)?

_____

17. Did Nicodemus yet understand what Jesus was teaching him?

_____

18. What was Jesus' question, because of Nicodemus' response (*v.10*)?

     a. "Are you a _____ (*a teacher of Judaism*) of Israel?"

     b. "Do you not _____ these things?"

19. What else did Jesus proclaim to Nicodemus in truth (*v.11*)?

     a. "We speak that we do _____..."

     b. "We _____ (*to bear witness*) that we have seen..."

20. What did the Pharisees do with the witness of Jesus (*v.11*)[39]?

_____

21. What did Jesus have to say about the Pharisees' lack of belief in Him (*v.12*)?

     a. They did not believe Him, when He told them about _____ things (*the work of God done on Earth to give men the new birth through His Spirit*)

     b. They would not believe Him, if He told them about _____ things (*the purposes of God in Heaven to grant salvation to men through Jesus Christ*)

---

[38] *John 3:6* (lit.): **"That which is born of the natural man is a natural man and that which is born of the Spirit of God is spirit."**
[39] *John 3:11*: To not receive Jesus' witness means *to not believe Jesus' testimony*

22. What man has ascended into Heaven, according to Jesus (***v.13***)[40]?

_____

23. Who is He that came down from Heaven (***v.13***)[41]?

_____

24. Where did Jesus state He was (***v.13***)[42]?

_____

25. What did Moses do in the wilderness (***v.14***)?

_____

26. In like manner, what had to happen to Jesus (***v.14***)[43]?

_____

27. Why did this have to happen to Jesus (***v.15***)[44]?

_____

28. Who did God love (*to have godly love toward*) (***v.16***)[45]?

_____

29. Because God loved the world, what did He do (***v.16***)[46]?

_____

30. Why did God do this (***v.16***)?

_____

31. How do we gain everlasting life (***v.16***)[47]?

_____

32. Why did God send His Son into the world (***v.17***)?

    a. Not to _____ (*to inflict a penalty upon*) the world

    b. That the world through Him might be _____

33. How can we be saved (*to obtain salvation from sin*) (***v.17***)?

_____

---

[40] ***John 3:13***: To have ascended to Heaven means *to have dwelt in Heaven to learn the mysteries of God*

[41] ***John 3:13b***: To descend from Heaven speaks of *one who previously made Heaven His abode* (Jesus Christ)

[42] ***John 3:13c***: For the Son of Man to be both on Earth and in Heaven speaks of *His deity (omnipresence) and perpetual presence in the bosom of the Father* (cf. ***John 1:18***)

[43] ***John 3:14***: To be lifted up speaks of *the elevation of Jesus on the cross*

[44] ***John 3:15***: To perish means *to lose eternal life and inherit eternal misery*

[45] ***John 3:16***: The world means *the inhabitants of the world*

[46] ***John 3:16b***: God giving His Son means that *God gave His Son to us to take care of our needs*

[47] ***John 3:16c***: To believe in Jesus means *to put one's trust in Him*

34. Who are those that are not condemned (*v.18*)?

_____

35. Who are those that are condemned already (*now*) (*v.18*)?

_____

36. Why are these people condemned already (*v.18*)?

_____

37. What is the condemnation (*the damnatory judgment of God*) (*v.19*)?

    a. _____ (*the saving truth embodied in Christ and, by His love and effort, imparted to mankind*) is come into the world

    b. Men loved _____ (*ignorance of divine things and human duties; especially regarding God's salvation*), rather than _____

38. Why did men love darkness more than light (*v.19*)?

_____

39. What is true about every person that does evil (*to commit acts of sin*) (*v.20*)?

    a. They _____ the light

    b. They do not _____ (*to submit oneself to*) to the light

40. Why do these people not do these things (*v.20*)[48]?

_____

41. What is true about those that do truth (*to act uprightly*) (*v.21*)?

_____

42. Why do these people submit themselves to the light (*v.21*)[49]?

_____

43. Why are these people not ashamed of their deeds (*v.21*)[50]?

_____

44. Where did Jesus and His disciples go after these things (*v.22*)?

_____

45. What did Jesus do in this place (*v.22*)?

    a. He _____ (*to stay*) with them

    b. He _____ (*to immerse*)

_____

[48] *John 3:20*: To have one's deeds be reproved is *to have one's deeds exposed to be sinful*
[49] *John 3:21*: To have one's deeds to be made manifest is *to reveal them*
[50] *John 3:21b*: To be wrought in God means *to have work done in God* (as opposed to the flesh or sinful things)

46. Who was also baptizing (*v.23*)?

_____

47. Where was he doing this (*v.23*)[51]?

_____

48. Why did he baptize there (*v.23*)?

_____

49. What did the people do when they learned that John baptized there (*v.23*)?

    a. They _____

    b. They were _____ (*to immerse*)

50. What had not yet happened to John the Baptist (*v.24*)?

_____

51. What arose between John's disciples and the Jews (*v.25*)?

_____

52. What was the question about (*v.25*)[52]?

_____

53. What title did these people give to John the Baptist (*v.26*)[53]?

_____

54. What did these people call Jesus (*v.26*)?

_____

55. What did John do regarding Jesus (*v.26*)?

_____

56. What was Jesus doing, to make them question (*v.26*)?

_____

57. What was happening as He did this (*v.26*)?

_____

58. What did John say about a man's work for God (*v.27*)[54]?

_____

59. To truly do a work for God, do we need God's approval first (*v.27*)?

_____

---

[51] *John 3:23*: Aenon was an area west of the Jordan River
[52] *John 3:25*: The question of purifying revolved around the practice of baptism
[53] *John 3:26*: Rabbi was *an honorific title for Teacher*
[54] *John 3:27*: To receive means *to procure or claim for oneself*

60. What had these people heard John bear witness (*to testify*) of before (*v.28*)?

     a. That he said, "I am not the _____ (*the Messiah*)."

     b. That he said, "I am sent _____ Him."

61. Who is he that has the bride (*v.29*)[55]?

_____

62. Does the friend of the bridegroom have the bride (*v.29*)[56]?

_____

63. What does the friend of the bridegroom do (*v.29*)?

     a. He _____ (*to stand near to a person*)

     b. He _____ the bridegroom

     c. He _____ greatly, because of the bridegroom's voice

64. Did John the Baptist see himself as the bridegroom or his friend (*v.29*)?

_____

65. Who did John the Baptist say that Jesus was (*v.28-29*)?

_____

66. Because the bridegroom had come, what happened to John, when he saw Him work and heard His voice preach the Gospel (*v.29*)[57]?

_____

67. What was John's response to Jesus' presence and ministry (*v.30*)?

     a. "He must _____ (*to grow in authority as a teacher and in the number of followers*)."

     b. "I must _____ (*to decrease in authority and popularity*)."

68. What is true about Him that comes from above (*from Heaven*) (*v.31*)[58]?

_____

69. What did John the Baptist state about those that are of Earth (*v.31*)?

     a. They are _____ (*to have a human origin and earthly nature*)

     b. They _____ of the earth (*to have an earthly style of speech*)

---

[55] **John 3:29**: The bridegroom is *a newly married man or one about to be married*
[56] **John 3:29b**: The friend of the bridegroom goes on his behalf to ask the hand of the bride and render the bridegroom with various services in order to close the marriage
[57] **John 3:29c**: For one's joy to be fulfilled means that *their joy is complete in every particular*
[58] **John 3:31**: Being above all speaks of *Jesus' being greater in dignity and power than any on Earth*

70. What is true about Him that comes from Heaven (**v.31**)?

_____

71. What did Jesus testify (_to bear witness of_) to the world about (**v.32**)?

      a. What He had _____ (_to experience_) in Heaven

      b. What He had _____ in Heaven

72. Who received (_to believe_) the testimony of Jesus (**v.32**)?

_____

73. What happened to those that do believe in Jesus' testimony (**v.33**)[59]?

_____

74. What is true about one that God has sent (**v.34**)[60]?

_____

75. Why is this true (**v.34**)[61]?

_____

76. What things are true about God the Father (**v.35**)?

      a. He _____ the Son

      b. He has _____ all things into His hand (_to commit to one's_

      protecting and upholding power)

77. Who has everlasting life (**v.36**)?

_____

78. Who shall not see life (_everlasting life_) (**v.36**)?

_____

79. Instead of seeing eternal life, what will happen to this person (**v.36**)[62]?

_____

---

[59] **John 3:32**: To set to his seal is _to confirm something for oneself_ (in this case: whoever believes the words of Christ is also believing the words of God, which are all true)

[60] **John 3:33**: To speak the words of God means _to speak what God bids him to say_

[61] **John 3:34**: To not give the Spirit by measure means _to not give the Spirit sparingly to one_ (speaking of Jesus)

[62] **John 3:36**: The wrath of God is _the anger of God at sin, which reveals itself through everlasting punishment that remains on that person forever_

Meditation (What God Spoke to Me About):

_____

_____

_____

_____

_____

_____

_____

Application (How I Can Apply What I Learned):

_____

_____

_____

_____

_____

_____

_____

_____

_____

Memorization (How I Can Retain What I Read):

Suggestions: *John 3:3-7; 3:14-18; 3:30; 3:36*

_____

_____

_____

Assessment (How I Am Doing With My Application and Memorization):

_____

_____

_____

_____

_____

Bible Study Questions (*John 4:1-54*)

Instructions: Pray that God will help you to understand this passage. Read through this Bible passage twice: once for reading and another time for understanding. After reading, consider and answer the questions listed below. Write down notes regarding anything else God spoke to you about.

1. What did the Pharisees hear about Jesus (*v.1*)?

       a. He _____ more disciples than John the Baptist

       b. He _____ (*to immerse*) more disciples than John the Baptist

2. Who did the baptizing, Jesus or His disciples (*v.2*)?

_____

3. What did Jesus do, when He heard what the Pharisees knew (*v.3*)?

       a. He left _____

       b. He departed again to _____

4. Why did Jesus travel through Samaria (*v.4*)[63]?

_____

5. What city did Jesus and His disciples come to in Samaria (*v.5*)?

_____

6. Where was this city located (*v.5*)[64]?

_____

7. What was also located in this city (*v.6*)?

_____

8. Why did Jesus sit on the well (*v.6*)?

_____

9. About what time did this occur (*v.6*)[65]?

_____

10. Who came out to the well to draw water (*v.7*)?

_____

11. What did Jesus say to her (*v.7*)?

_____

---

[63] **John 4:4**: To must needs means *to be necessary, because of circumstances or the conduct of others*
[64] **John 4:5**: cf. **Genesis 33:19; 48:22**
[65] **John 4:6**: The sixth hour is about noon

12. Where were Jesus' disciples at this time (**v.8**)[66]?

_____

13. Why was this woman so surprised at Jesus' request (**v.9**)[67]?

_____

14. What two things did Jesus say the woman did not know (**v.10**)?

     a. The _____ of God that could be offered

     b. Who it was that said to her, "Give me to _____."

15. If this woman knew who Jesus was and the gift He offered, what would she have asked Him to give to her (**v.10**)[68]?

_____

16. What title did this woman give Jesus, at this time (**v.11**)[69]?

_____

17. What was the woman's response to Jesus' statement (**v.11-12**)?

     a. "You have _____ to draw (*to draw water from a well*) with…"

     b. "The well is _____…"

     c. "From where do you have that _____ water?"

     d. "Are you _____ than our father Jacob?" (**v.12**)

18. Was Jesus greater than Jacob (**v.12**)?

_____

19. What things did Jacob do for the Samaritan people (**v.12**)?

     a. He _____ them (*to supply*) the well

     b. He _____ from the well himself, with his children and cattle

20. What did Jesus say would happen to whomever drank out of Jacob's well (**v.13**)?

_____

21. What did Jesus say would happen to whomever drank of the water He gave them (**v.14**)?

_____

22. What would that water be inside the person that drank of the water Jesus gave them (**v.14**)?

_____

---

[66] **John 4:8**: Meat means *food or nourishment*
[67] **John 4:9**: The Samaritans were a group of half-breeds that were part-Hebrew and part-Gentile. They were rejected by the Jews, because of their breeding and often went out of their way to avoid them
[68] **John 4:10**: Living water is figurative of the spirit and truth of God, as satisfying the needs of our souls
[69] **John 4:11**: Sir was a title of distinction given to honor a person

23. What would that water do inside the person that drank of the water Jesus gave them (**v.14**)[70]?

_____

24. When a person drinks of the water of God's Truth, what does it eventually bring forth (**v.14**)?

_____

25. What was the woman's response to Jesus' message (**v.15**)?

_____

26. Why did she want the water Jesus offered (**v.15**)?

    a. So she would not _____

    b. So she would not have to come to the well to _____

27. Did she understand what Jesus was really speaking of?

_____

28. I think she thought Jesus was offering (**circle one**):   **Physical living water**   **Spiritual living water**

29. What did Jesus then tell her to do (**v.16**)?

    a. "_____..."

    b. "...Call your _____..."

    c. "...and _____ back here."

30. What was her answer to Jesus' command (**v.17**)?

_____

31. Did Jesus already know that she did not have a husband (**v.17-18**)?

_____

32. Did Jesus commend her for telling the truth to Him (**v.17**)?

_____

33. How many husbands had this woman had (**v.18**)?

_____

34. Was the man she was with at that time her husband (**v.18**)?

_____

35. What was the woman's observation of Jesus at that point (**v.19**)[71]?

_____

---

[70] **John 4:14**: To spring up means _to gush up_

[71] **John 4:19**: A prophet means _one who was filled with God's Spirit and revealed supernatural knowledge about previously hidden things_

36. Where did she say their fathers worshipped God (**v.20**)[72]?

_____

37. Where did the Jews say that men ought to worship (**v.20**)?

_____

38. Where did Jesus say that God would eventually be worshipped (**v.21**)?

       a. Eventually not in that _____

       b. Eventually not in _____

39. What is another name for God mentioned by Jesus (**v.21**)?

_____

40. What did Jesus say about the Samaritans' worship (**v.22**)?

_____

41. What did Jesus say about the Jews' worship (**v.22**)?

_____

42. Why did the Jews know what they worshipped (**v.22**)[73]?

_____

43. What did Jesus have to say about the hour (_a definite time_) of true worship (**v.23**)?

       a. It was _____ (_to occur at a future date_)

       b. It _____ (_to occur in the present time_)

44. Who would come to worship the Father (**v.23**)[74]?

_____

45. How would these worshippers worship the Father (**v.23**)?

       a. In _____ (_communication through the third part of man: the spirit_)

       b. In _____ (_the absolute Truth of God's Word_)

46. Who seeks these sort of worshippers to worship Him (**v.23**)?

_____

47. What form is God the Father (**v.24**)?

_____

_____

---

[72] **John 4:20**: The mountain mentioned in Mount Gerizim, where the Samaritans worshipped, because of the Jews' prejudice against them, until it was destroyed in 129BC

[73] **John 4:22**: Salvation being of the Jews means that _the means for salvation came forth from the Jews_ (Jesus)

[74] **John 4:23**: True worshippers are _perfect , approved, and strong in their worship of God_

48. If we are to worship God, how must He be worshipped (**v.24**)?

      a. In _____ (*communication through the third part of man: the spirit*)

      b. In _____ (*the absolute Truth of God's Word*)

49. If we do not worship God this way, are we worshipping God at all (**v.24**)?

_____

50. Must God be worshipped this way, if we are to truly worship Him (**v.24**)?

_____

51. Who did the woman say that she knew was coming (**v.25**)?

_____

52. What is another name for this person (**v.25**)?

_____

53. What did she say this man would tell them, when He came (**v.25**)?

_____

54. What was Jesus' response to her (**v.26**)?

_____

55. Who was Jesus claiming to be before this woman (**v.25-26**)?

_____

56. When Jesus told her this, who came back to Jesus (**v.27**)?

_____

57. What did they marvel (*to wonder*) at (**v.27**)?

_____

58. What did they not say to Jesus (**v.27**)?

      a. "What do you _____?"

      b. "Why do you _____ with her?"

59. What was the woman's response to Jesus' words (**v.28**)?

      a. She _____ her water pot

      b. She went her way (*to depart*) into the _____

60. What did she say to the men of the city about Jesus (**v.29**)?

      a. "_____, see a man…"

      b. "He _____ me all things that ever I did…"

      c. "…Is this not the _____?"

61. Do you think this woman was excited to discover that Jesus was the Christ?

_____

62. Do you think her excitement caused her to tell others about Jesus?

_____

63. What impact should this woman's example make in your life?

_____

64. What happened, when the woman told the men about Jesus (*v.30*)?

      a. They _____ out of the city

      b. They _____ unto Jesus

65. While this woman was in the city, what did Jesus' disciples ask Him to do (*v.31*)?

_____

66. What was Jesus' response (*v.32*)[75] [76]?

_____

67. What did the disciples then ask one another (*v.33*)?

_____

68. Did the disciples understand what Jesus was telling them (*v.33*)?

_____

69. What did Jesus say nourished His soul (*v.34*)?

      a. To do the _____ (*commands*) of Him that _____ Him

      b. To _____ (*to carry through completely*) His work

70. Do you have these same desires concerning your walk with God?

_____

71. What did the Jews say about the harvest (*v.35*)?

_____

72. What did Jesus tell His disciples about the harvest of souls (*v.35*)?

      a. "Lift up your _____..."

      b. "_____ on the fields."

73. Why did He tell them to do this (*v.35*)[77]?

_____

_____

[75] **John 4:32**: The meat that Jesus speaks of is *the nourishment of the soul; not the body*

[76] **John 4:24b**: That you know not of means *that you cannot perceive with your eyes*

[77] **John 4:35**: The whiteness of the harvest speaks of *the whitening color of ripening grain*

74. What do they that reap the harvest of souls receive (**v.36**)[78]?

     a. They receive _____ (*reward*)

     b. They gather _____ unto life eternal

75. When the wages and fruit are gained from the harvest, who gets to rejoice in it (**v.36**)?

     a. He that _____ (*to sow the seed of God's Word*)

     b. He that _____ (*to gather the fruit of the seed together*)

76. What saying does Jesus state is true (**v.37**) [79]?

_____

77. What did Jesus do to the disciples (**v.38**)?

_____

78. Where were they sent to do this (**v.38**)[80]?

_____

79. Who labored for this harvest of souls, instead of the disciples (**v.38**)?

_____

80. Because they did the reaping work, what were the disciples doing (**v.38**)[81]?

_____

81. Who is greater, the person that sows or reaps (*I Corinthians 3:7-8*)?

_____

82. What happened to the Samaritans of that city (**v.39**)?

_____

83. Why did they do this (**v.39**)?

_____

84. How many of the Samaritans believed, because of this (**v.39**)?

_____

85. If God used the testimony of one woman, could He use your testimony the same way?

_____

86. When the Samaritans came to Jesus, what did they ask Him to do (**v.40**)?

_____

_____

[78] **John 4:36**: To gather fruit unto life eternal speaks of *those, who by their labor of preaching the Gospel, have fitted souls to receive eternal life*

[79] **John 4:36b**: This idea of sowing and reaping is proverbial and refers to one doing the work and another reaping the fruit of the work of another. Both worked and both are able rejoice in the fruits of their labor.

[80] **John 4:38**: To bestow no labor means *they did not toil to ensure a harvest would be available*

[81] **John 4:38b**: To enter into their labors means *they entered into the toilsome work alongside the others*

87. How long did Jesus stay with them (*v.40*)?

_____

88. Because Jesus stayed with them, what else happened (*v.41*)?

_____

89. Why did they do this (*v.41*)[82]?

_____

90. Why did the townspeople tell the woman that they believed Jesus (*v.42*)?

      a. Not because of her _____ (*story*)

      b. They had _____ Him for themselves

      c. They knew that He was indeed the _____

91. What was one work of the Christ (*v.42*)[83]?

_____

92. After two days, where did Jesus depart to (*v.43*)?

_____

93. Why did Jesus go this place (*v.44*)[84]?

_____

94. What did the Galileans do, when Jesus came to them (*v.45*)?

_____

95. Why did they do this (*v.45*)[85]?

_____

96. How did they know what Jesus did (*v.45*)?

_____

97. What city in Galilee did Jesus come again to (*v.46*)?

_____

98. What special work did Jesus perform there (*v.46*)[86]?

_____

_____

[82] *John 4:41*: Believing because of His own Word means that *Jesus taught and the people believed His teachings*
[83] *John 4:42*: Jesus being the Savior of the world means that He is *the Messiah through whom God has provided salvation from sins*
[84] *John 4:44*: To have no honor meant that *Jesus would not be respected as a prophet in His own homeland*
[85] *John 4:45*: The events spoken of are found in *John 2:12-25*
[86] *John 4:46*: cf. *John 2:1-11*

99. Who had a son that was sick (**v.46**)[87]?

_____

100. Where did this man live (**v.46**)?

_____

101. What did this man do, when he heard that Jesus was in Galilee (**v.47**)?

     a. He _____ unto Him

     b. He _____ (_to request or beg_) Him

102. What did he ask Jesus to do for him (**v.47**)?

     a. To _____ down

     b. To _____ his son

103. Why did he ask Jesus to do this (**v.47**)?

_____

104. What did Jesus say the man needed to see, before he would believe in Him (**v.48**)[88]?

_____

105. What was the man's response (**v.49**)?

_____

106. Did this man need a sign or wonder to believe that Jesus could heal his son?

_____

107. Did this man believe that Jesus was powerful enough to heal his son?

_____

108. What did Jesus tell this man to do (**v.50**)?

_____

109. Why did Jesus tell him this (**v.50**)?

_____

110. When Jesus said this, what did the man do (**v.50**)?

     a. He _____ the word that Jesus had spoken to him

     b. He _____ his way

111. Who met the man as he traveled back home (**v.51**)?

_____

---

[87] **John 4:46b**: This nobleman was an officer or minister to a prince
[88] **John 4:48**: The signs and wonders spoken of are _those miracles performed by which God authenticates the men sent by Him_

112. What did they tell him about his son (**v.51**)?

_____

113. What did he ask his servants regarding his sons healing (**v.52**)[89]?

_____

114. When did the servants tell their master that the fever left his son (**v.52**)[90]?

_____

115. What did the father realize about his son's healing (**v.53**)?

_____

116. What happened as a result of Jesus' work (**v.53**)?

_____

117. What this the first, second, or third miracle that Jesus performed when He came out of Judaea and into Galilee (**v.54**)?

_____

---

[89] **John 4:52**: To amend means _to be better_ (in health)
[90] **John 4:52b**: The seventh hour is _about 1pm_

Meditation (What God Spoke to Me About):

_____

_____

_____

_____

_____

_____

_____

_____

Application (How I Can Apply What I Learned):

_____

_____

_____

_____

_____

_____

_____

_____

_____

Memorization (How I Can Retain What I Read):

Suggestions: _John 4:10; 4:13-14; 4:23-24; 4:28-29; 4:34-38_

_____

_____

_____

Assessment (How I Am Doing With My Application and Memorization):

_____

_____

_____

_____

_____

_____

Bible Study Questions (*John 5:1-47*)

Instructions: Pray that God will help you to understand this passage. Read through this Bible passage twice: once for reading and another time for understanding. After reading, consider and answer the questions listed below. Write down notes regarding anything else God spoke to you about.

1. After Jesus performed His second miracle, what special event took place (*v.1*)?

_____

2. Where did Jesus travel up to (*v.1*)?

_____

3. What was in Jerusalem by the sheep market (*v.2*)[91]?

_____

4. What was its name in the Hebrew language (*v.2*)?

_____

5. How many porches (*a covered series of columns arranged in a circle*) were there (*v.2*)?

_____

6. How many people lay inside these porches (*v.3*)?

_____

7. What sort of people made up this multitude (*v.3*)?

     a. _____ (*sick*) folk

     b. _____ folk

     c. _____ (*deprived of a foot, maimed*) folk

     d. _____ (*to have wasted members of the body*) folk

8. What were all these people doing at the pool (*v.3*)[92]?

_____

9. What sort of being caused the moving of the water (*v.4*)?

_____

10. What did this being do regarding the moving of the water (*v.4*)?

     a. It went down (*as from Heaven to Earth*) at a certain _____ (*from time to time*)

     b. It _____ (*to agitate*) the water

---

[91] *John 5:2*: The sheep market was the sheep gate
[92] *John 5:3*: Moving means *to be agitated*

11. What happened to the first person that entered the water, after it was troubled (**v.4**)?

_____

12. Who was present at the pool (**v.5**)?

_____

13. How long had he had his infirmity (*sickness*) (**v.5**)?

_____

14. Who saw the man lying on one of the porches (**v.6**)?

_____

15. What did He know about the man (**v.6**)?

_____

16. What did He ask the man (**v.6**)[93]?

_____

17. Who did the man have to help him get into the pool, when it was troubled (**v.7**)?

_____

18. What would happen to him, because of this (**v.7**)?

_____

19. What did Jesus tell this man in response (**v.8**)?

      a. To _____ (*to arise*)

      b. To _____ up (*to pick up and carry*) his bed (*a pallet that held one person*)

      c. To _____

20. What happened to the man (**v.9**)?

      a. He was made _____ (*to be restored to health*)

      b. He _____ up his bed

      c. He _____

21. How quickly was this man healed (**v.9**)?

_____

22. What day did Jesus heal this man on (**v.9**)?

_____

23. Because it was this day, what did the Jews say to the healed man (**v.10**)?

      a. "It is the _____ day."

      b. "It is not _____ for you to carry your bed."

_____

[93] **John 5:6**: To be made whole means *to be given a sound, healthy body*

24. Who did the man say told him to carry his bed (**v.11**)?

_____

25. What did the people ask about the one that told him to carry his bed (**v.12**)?

_____

26. Did the man know who healed him (**v.13**)?

_____

27. Why did he not know (**v.13**)[94]?

_____

28. Why did Jesus do this (**v.13**)?

_____

29. Who found the healed man later on (**v.14**)?

_____

30. Where did He find him (**v.14**)?

_____

31. What did Jesus say to the healed man (**v.14**)?

     a. "…You are made _____…"

     b. "…_____ no more…"

32. What did Jesus say would happen to the man, if he continued to sin (**v.14**)?

_____

33. What did the healed man do after Jesus spoke to him (**v.15**)?

     a. He _____

     b. He told the Jews that _____ made him whole

34. Because the man told the Jews this, what did they do to Jesus (**v.16**)?

     a. They _____ (*to harass and trouble*) Him

     b. They sought to _____ (*to kill*) Him

35. Why did they seek to do these things to Jesus (**v.16**)?

_____

36. What was Jesus' response to their persecution of Him (**v.17**)?

     a. "My Father _____ hitherto (*until now*)…"

     b. "Because He works, I _____."

---

[94] **John 5:13**: To be conveyed is *to be withdrawn away from a thing or person*

37. Because of Jesus' statement, what did the Jews seek the more to do (**v.18**)?

_____

38. Why did they want to do this to Jesus (**v.18**)?

      a. Because He had _____ (*to deprive of authority*) the Sabbath

      b. Because He said also that God was His _____

39. What was so special about Jesus' statement about His relationship with God (**v.18**)?

_____

40. Does this mean that Jesus Christ was also God in the flesh (**v.18; John 1:14**)?

_____

41. What true statements does Jesus make about His relationship with the Father (**v.19**)[95]?

      a. "The Son can do _____ of Himself…"

      b. "…the Son does what He sees the _____ do…"

      c. "…What things the Father does, these also do the _____ likewise."

42. Why did God the Father show (*to show works for Him to do*) Jesus everything that He was to do on Earth (**v.20**)[96]?

_____

43. What would God the Father show Jesus that He was to do during His ministry (**v.20**)?

_____

44. Why would the Father have the son perform such works (**v.20**)?

_____

45. What other works did Jesus say the Father performs (**v.21**)?

      a. He _____ up the dead (*to recall the dead to life*)

      b. He _____ the dead (*to restore to life*)

46. Since God the Father can do these works, what can the Son also do (**v.21**)?

_____

47. Was healing a lame man a great work of God?

_____

48. Would raising people from the dead be considered a greater work?

_____

---

[95] **John 5:19**: Jesus is explaining to the Jews the relationship of God the Father and Son: the Son is eternally submissive to the will of the Father and does what the Father does; instead of acting independently of the Father's will for the universe
[96] **John 5:20**: This sort of love is *an approving, friendly love*

49. Who does God the Father judge (*to condemn and inflict a penalty upon*) (**v.22**)?

_____

50. Who did the Father commit all judgment (*condemnation*) to (**v.22**)?

_____

51. Why did the Father do this (**v.23**)?

_____

52. If we honor God the Father, who else should we honor (**v.23**)?

_____

53. If we do not honor God the Son, who else are we not honoring (**v.23**)?

_____

54. Why is this true (**v.23**)?

_____

55. How does a person receive everlasting (*eternal*) life (**v.24**)[97]?

    a. If we _____ the words of Jesus Christ

    b. If we _____ on Him that sent Jesus Christ

56. In addition to having everlasting life, what is true regarding those that believe on Jesus (**v.24**)?

    a. They shall not come into _____ (*damnatory judgment*)

    b. They are passed from _____ unto _____

57. What things did Jesus truthfully say would occur and were occurring at that time (**v.25**)?

    a. The _____ (*spiritually dead*) would hear the voice of the Son of God

    b. Those that _____ (*to yield in obedience to the voice*) would live (*to become spiritually alive*)

58. Why does the Son of God have this power (**v.26**)?

    a. The Father has _____ in Himself (*the absolute fullness of life; as part of the nature of God*)

    b. The Father has given (*to grant*) to the Son to have _____ in Himself

59. What else has God granted unto the Lord Jesus (**v.27**)?

_____

_____

[97] **John 5:24**: To believe on Him that sent Jesus Christ means *to believe and embrace what God has made known through Christ or concerning Him*

60. Why has God granted this to Jesus (**v.27**)[98]?

_____

61. What did Jesus tell the people to not do regarding His words (**v.28**)?

_____

62. What did Jesus say was coming in the future (**v.28-29**)?

       a. All that are in the _____ would hear His voice

       b. They will also come _____ (*to be physically resurrected*) (**v.29**)

63. What would those that have done good come forth unto (**v.29**)[99]?

_____

64. What would those that have done evil come forth unto (**v.29**)[100]?

_____

65. What does Jesus do of His own self (*to act according to His own will*) (**v.30**)?

_____

66. What does Jesus do as He hears (*to hear instruction from the Father*) (**v.30**)[101]?

_____

67. What is special about Jesus' judgment (**v.30**)?

_____

68. Why is this so (**v.30**)?

       a. He does not seek His own _____ (*what one wishes to be done*)

       b. He seeks the _____ of the Father which sent Him

69. What would be true about Jesus, if he bore witness (*to testify*) of Himself (**v.31**)[102]?

_____

70. Why did Jesus not have to bear witness of Himself (**v.32**)?

_____

71. Was this man's witness of Jesus true or false (**v.32**)?

_____

_____

[98] **John 5:27**: The Son of Man is one of the Messianic titles of Christ, speaking specifically of His full humanity; whereas the title of being the Son of God speaks of His full deity

[99] **John 5:29**: This resurrection of life speaks of *the reward for all those that believe in Jesus, allowing their good works done in Jesus' name to be rewarded* (cf. **I Thessalonians 4**)

[100] **John 5:29b**: The resurrection of damnation speaks of *the resurrection of those that did not believe in Jesus Christ at the Great White Throne Judgment, which occurs at the end of time* (cf. **Revelation 20**)

[101] **John 5:30**: This judgment is *the absolute judgment of Christ regarding the righteousness or unrighteousness of men*

[102] **John 5:31**: To bear witness of oneself means *to testify of one's own self* (especially their own goodness)

72. What was the man's name that bore witness of Jesus (*v.33*)?

_____

73. What sort of witness did this man give to the Jews (*v.33*)?

_____

74. Did Jesus really care about what John said about Him (*v.34*)?

_____

75. Do you think Jesus cared more about what God thought of Him or what John did?

_____

76. Do you think we ought to care more about what God thinks of us or what others do?

_____

77. Why did Jesus then tell the Jews about John's testimony of Him (*v.34*)?

_____

78. What did Jesus say about John the Baptist (*v.35*)?

    a. He was a burning _____ (*a light that showed the right way*)

    b. He was a shining _____

79. What did Jesus say the Jews were willing to do regarding John the Baptist (*v.35*)[103]?

_____

80. What was Jesus' witness compared to that of John the Baptist's (*v.36*)?

_____

81. Why was this true (*v.36*)?

    a. The Father gave Jesus works to _____ (*to accomplish*)

    b. Jesus did those _____ (*the acts of Christ to rouse men to*

    believe in Him)

    c. The works of Christ bore _____ of Him that the Father had

    _____ Him

82. Who else bore witness of Jesus Christ (*v.37*)?

_____

83. What special act did He perform (*v.37*)?

_____

_____

[103] *John 5:35* (lit.): *"You were willing to rejoice while his light shone."*

84. What was true about the Jews' relationship with God (**v.37-38**)?

      a. They had not _____ His _____ at any time

      b. They had not _____ His shape (*figure or form*)

      c. They did not have His _____ abiding in them (**v.38**)

85. How did Jesus know this to be true (**v.38**)?

_____

86. What did Jesus command the people to do (**v.39**)?

_____

87. Why did Jesus command them to do this (**v.39-40**)?

      a. Because they thought that had _____ through the scriptures

      b. Because the scriptures _____ (*to bear witness*) of Jesus

      c. Because they would not _____ to Jesus (*to commit oneself to the*

      instruction of Jesus and enter into fellowship with Him) that they might have _____

      (*eternal life*) (**v.40**)

88. Who did Jesus not receive honor (*to seek after glory*) from (**v.41**)?

_____

89. Should we seek honor from God or from men (**v.41**)?

_____

90. What did Jesus know about the Jews (**v.42**)?

_____

91. How did Jesus know this (**v.43**)[104]?

_____

92. What did Jesus say would happen if a person came in His own name to the Jews (**v.43**)[105]?

_____

93. What did Jesus say kept the Jews from believing in Him (**v.44**)[106]?

      a. They received (*to strive to obtain*) _____ (*praise*) one of another

      b. They did not seek (*to strive after*) the _____ (*praise*) that came

      from God only

94. Should we strive after praise from God or praise from men (**v.44**)?

_____

[104] **John 5:43**: To come in His Father's name means *to come on His Father's behalf to promote His cause*
[105] **John 5:43b**: To receive means *to receive with the intention of obeying*
[106] **John 5:44**: The Jews cared more about what men thought about them than what God did

95. Despite their attitude, what did Jesus say He would not do to the Jews (**v.45**)[107]?

_____

96. Who did Jesus say would accuse them (**v.45**)[108]?

_____

97. What attitude did the Jews have toward this man (**v.45**)?

_____

98. What did Jesus say would have happened, if the Jews believed Moses (**v.46**)?

_____

99. Why is this true (**v.46**)?

_____

100. Did Jesus say the Jews truly believed Moses' writings or not (**v.47**)?

_____

101. If the Jews did not believe Moses, what else could they not do (**v.47**)?

_____

---

[107] **John 5:45**: This accusation speaks of an _making an accusation that is not legally authorized by God_
[108] **John 5:45b**: When Jesus speaks of Moses, He speaks of _the first five books of the Bible_ (Moses' writings)

Meditation (What God Spoke to Me About):

_____
_____
_____
_____
_____
_____
_____
_____

Application (How I Can Apply What I Learned):

_____
_____
_____
_____
_____
_____
_____
_____

Memorization (How I Can Retain What I Read):

Suggestions: *John 5:6-8; 5:16-19; 5:24; 5:30-32; 5:39*

_____
_____
_____

Assessment (How I Am Doing With My Application and Memorization):

_____
_____
_____
_____
_____
_____

Bible Study Questions (*John 6:1-71*)

Instructions: Pray that God will help you to understand this passage. Read through this Bible passage twice: once for reading and another time for understanding. After reading, consider and answer the questions listed below. Write down notes regarding anything else God spoke to you about.

1. After Jesus preached to the Jews in Jerusalem, what did He go over (*v.1*)?

_____

2. What is another name for this body of water (*v.1*)[109]?

_____

3. Who followed after Jesus (*v.2*)?

_____

4. Why did they do this (*v.2*)?

_____

5. Where did Jesus go up into (*v.3*)?

_____

6. What did He do there (*v.3*)?

_____

7. Who did He do this with (*v.3*)?

_____

8. What special time was near (*v.4*)?

_____

9. What was one thing that marked it as a special time (*v.4*)?

_____

10. What did Jesus see, when He lifted up His eyes (*v.5*)?

_____

11. Who did Jesus speak to (*v.5*)?

_____

12. What did Jesus ask him (*v.5*)?

_____

---

[109] *John 6:1*: This was named so by Herod Antipas (governor of Galilee) in honor of Tiberius Caesar

13. Why did Jesus ask him this (**v.6**)[110]?

_____

14. Did Jesus need to ask Philip or did He already know what to do (**v.6**)?

_____

15. What was Philip's answer to Jesus (**v.7**)[111]?

_____

16. Who came while Philip and Jesus were talking (**v.8**)?

_____

17. Who was this man's brother (**v.8**)?

_____

18. What did he have to say (**v.9**)?

      a. "There is a _____ (*a little boy*) here…"

      b. "He has _____ barley loaves and _____

      small fishes…"

      c. "But, what are they among so _____?"

19. Did Philip or Andrew believe that Jesus could provide them with food (**v.5-9**)?

_____

20. What did Jesus command His disciples to do (**v.10**)?

_____

21. What existed in the place that Jesus taught the people (**v.10**)?

_____

22. Because of this, what did the men do (**v.10**)?

_____

23. About how many men were present with Jesus (**v.10**)?

_____

24. What did Jesus do next (**v.11**)?

      a. He took the _____

      b. He gave _____ (*to give thanks to God before food is eaten*)

      c. He _____ (*to divide among several*) to the disciples

_____

[110] **John 6:6**: To prove means *to test for the purpose of making certain the quality of a person: what they think and how they will behave in a certain situation*

[111] **John 6:7**: Two hundred pennyworth was the equivalent of two hundred day's salary (two hundred denarii)

25. What did the disciples do with the loaves (**v.11**)[112]?

_____

26. What did Jesus and the disciples do the same things with (**v.11**)?

_____

27. How much were the people allowed to have (**v.11**)?

_____

28. How much did the people eat (**v.12**)?

_____

29. What did Jesus then tell His disciples to do (**v.12**)[113]?

_____

30. Why were they to do this (**v.12**)[114]?

_____

31. Because of Jesus' command, what did the disciples do (**v.13**)?

    a. They _____ them together

    b. They _____ twelve baskets with the fragments of the

    _____ barley loaves

32. Did Jesus give them just enough food or over and above what they needed (**v.13**)?

_____

33. When the men saw the miracle Jesus performed, what did they say about Him (**v.14**)[115]?

_____

34. Because of the sayings of the men, what did Jesus perceive (*to understand*) they would do (**v.15**)?

    a. That they would take Him by _____ (*to seize and carry off speedily*)

    b. That they would make Him a _____

35. Because of this, what did Jesus do (**v.15**)?

_____

36. Were Jesus' disciples with Him when He did this (**v.15**)?

_____

_____

[112] **John 6:11**: To be set down means *to sit down and dine together*
[113] **John 6:12**: The fragments were *remnants of food that were left over*
[114] **John 6:12b**: To be lost means *to spoil or vanish* (as food spoils)
[115] **John 6:14**: For Jesus to be "that prophet" means *the men called Jesus the Messiah*

37. Where did Jesus' disciples go (**v.16**)[116]?

_____

38. At what time did they go there (**v.16**)[117]?

_____

39. What did they do when they got there (**v.17**)?

      a. They entered into a _____

      b. They went over the _____

40. Where did they head toward (**v.17**)?

_____

41. What had happened as they travelled (**v.17-18**)?

      a. It was _____

      b. Jesus was not _____ to them

      c. The sea _____ (*to become agitated*), because of a great

      _____ (*a tempestuous wind*) that blew (**v.18**)

42. What did they see, after they had rowed twenty-five or thirty furlongs (*about three miles*) (**v.19**)?

      a. They saw Jesus _____ on the sea

      b. They saw Jesus _____ nigh (*to come near*) to the ship

43. What were the disciples' responses when they saw Jesus (**v.19**)?

_____

44. What did Jesus say to them (**v.20**)?

      a. "It is _____..."

      b. "...Be not _____."

45. What did the disciples do in response (**v.21**)?

_____

46. What happened to them when they did this (**v.21**)?

_____

_____

---

[116] **John 6:16**: The sea speaks of *the Sea of Galilee*
[117] **John 6:16b**: Even means *evening* (from 6pm to the beginning of nightfall)

47. What happened the following day (**v.22**)?

        a. The people stood on the other side of the _____

        b. They saw that there were no other _____ there

        c. They knew that Jesus had not gone with His disciples into their _____

        d. They knew that the disciples had gone away _____

48. Who did the only boat that was where Jesus taught belong to (**v.22**)?

_____

49. What came near to the place Jesus taught (**v.23**)?

_____

50. Where were these from (**v.23**)[118]?

_____

51. When the people could not find Jesus or His disciples, what did they do (**v.24**)?

        a. They took _____ (*to go into a ship*)

        b. They came to _____

52. Why did they do this (**v.24**)?

_____

53. Where did they find Jesus (**v.25**)?

_____

54. What did they ask Him (**v.25**)[119]?

_____

55. Why did Jesus say the people sought Him out (**v.26**)?

        a. Not because they saw the _____

        b. Because they ate of the _____

        c. Because they were _____ by them

56. What did Jesus command the people to labor for (*to earn by working*) (**v.27**)?

        a. Not for the meat (*food that nourishes the body*) which _____

(*to decompose*)

        b. For the meat (*food that nourishes the soul*) that _____

(*to continue to exist*) unto everlasting life

---

[118] **John 6:23**: Tiberius was a large city that lay close to the Sea of Galilee
[119] **John 6:25** (lit): "**Teacher, when did you come here?**"

57. Who gives the food that nourishes the soul (**v.27**)?

_____

58. Why can He do this (**v.27**)[120]?

_____

59. What did the people want Jesus to help them to do (**v.28**)[121]?

_____

60. Do you think we all ought to have the desire to do what God wishes us to do?

_____

61. What did Jesus answer was the work of God (*a work required and approved by God*) (**v.29**)?

_____

62. Do you think we can serve God until we have believed on His Son (**v.28-29**)?

_____

63. What two things did the people then ask Jesus, that they would see and believe in Him (**v.30**)?

    a. "What _____ (*a wonder or miracle*) do you show then?"

    b. "What _____ do you do (*to bring a thing to pass*)?"

64. Why did they ask Jesus for such things (**v.31**)[122]?

_____

65. What did they believe Moses gave them from Heaven to eat (**v.31**)?

_____

66. What had Jesus just given the people to eat miraculously (**v.9-14**)?

_____

67. What did Jesus say about the miracle of the bread from Heaven (**v.32**)?

    a. _____ did not give them the bread from Heaven

    b. His _____ gives them the true bread (*that which nourishes the soul unto life everlasting*) from Heaven

---

[120] **John 6:27**: To be sealed means *to be confirmed or authenticated* (in this case: God confirms the Son's testimony to the world that Jesus is who He professes to be)

[121] **John 6:28**: To work the works of God means *to have the strength to do what God wishes to be done*

[122] **John 6:31**: Fathers means *ancestors* (cf. **Exodus 16; Psalm 78**)

68. Who is the bread of God (*v.33*)[123]?

      a. He that came down from _____

      b. He that gives _____ (*eternal life*) unto the world

69. What then did the Jews ask Jesus to do (*v.34*)?

_____

70. Do you think they thought this was special bread they could eat and gain eternal life from?

_____

71. Who did Jesus plainly say He was (*v.35*)?

_____

72. What did Jesus say would happen to those that came to Him (*to commit oneself to the instruction of Christ and enter into fellowship with Him*) (*v.35*)[124]?

_____

73. What did Jesus say would happen to those that believed on Him (*v.35*)[125]?

_____

74. What had Jesus said to this group of people (*v.36*)?

      a. They had _____ Him (*to see Him exhibit the proofs of His Messiahship*)

      b. They did not _____ in Him

75. Who did Jesus say would come to Him (*to become His follower*) (*v.37*)[126]?

_____

76. What did Jesus say that He would do to those that came to Him (*v.37*)[127]?

_____

77. Why did Jesus say that He would not do this (*v.38*)?

      a. He did not come from _____ to do His own will (*desires*)

      b. He came from _____ to do the will of Him that sent Him

---

[123] **John 6:33**: Jesus calls Himself the Bread that came down from Heaven; this title means that *He is the divine Word, come from Heaven, who contains in Himself the source of heavenly life and supplies spiritual nourishment to souls; that they may attain to eternal life* (in short: eternal life comes from Jesus Christ alone)

[124] **John 6:35**: To never hunger means *to lack nothing required for a true spiritual life and salvation*

[125] **John 6:35b**: To never thirst means *to lack nothing required for the refreshment or strengthening of the soul*

[126] **John 6:37**: To give means *to give to someone to be a follower of them*

[127] **John 6:37b**: To cast out means *to deprive of the power and influence that Jesus exercises on the world*

78. What did Jesus say the Father's will was in sending Jesus to Earth (**v.39**)?

    a. That He should lose _____ of all the Father gave Him

    b. That He would _____ it up again (*to raise one up from death*) at the

    last day (*the day of Jehovah, when judgment is brought and the Kingdom is established*)

79. What is the will of Him that sent Jesus (**v.40**)?

_____

80. How does one receive everlasting life (**v.40**)?

    a. They _____ (*to look upon one with respect*) the Son

    b. They _____ on Him

81. What will happen to those that obtain everlasting life and pass from this earth (**v.40**)?

_____

82. Why did the Jews murmur (*to grumble in a low tone*) against Jesus (**v.41**)?

_____

83. Why did the Jews murmur about this fact (**v.42**)?

    a. They thought Jesus was the son of _____

    b. They thought they knew Jesus' _____ and mother

84. Because of these things, what could the Jews not understand (**v.42**)?

_____

85. What did Jesus command them to do with their murmuring (**v.43**)?

_____

86. Who did Jesus say could come (to come in belief) to Him (**v.44**)?

_____

87. What is the only way a person comes to Jesus (**v.44**)[128]?

_____

88. What will happen to those that come to Jesus (**v.44**)?

_____

89. What truth was written in the prophets (**v.45**)[129]?

_____

_____

---

[128] **John 6:44**: To draw means *to draw by inward power or lead one* (in this case: to believe in Jesus)
[129] **John 6:45**: cf. **Isaiah 54:13**

90. Who are those that come to Jesus (**v.45**)?

     a. Those that have _____ (*to perceive in the soul the inward*

     communication of God)

     b. Those that have _____ (*to increase in knowledge; especially of*

     Christ) from the Father

91. What man has seen (*to observe*) the Father (**v.46**)?

_____

92. Who is the only one that has seen the Father (**v.46**)?

_____

93. What true statement did Jesus give to the unbelieving Jews (**v.47**)?

_____

94. How does someone receive everlasting life (**v.47**)?

_____

95. What did Jesus say that He was (**v.48**)[130]?

_____

96. What did the Jews' fathers eat in the wilderness (**v.49**)?

_____

97. What happen to them (**v.49**)?

_____

98. What was special about the bread that came down from Heaven (**v.50**)?

     a. That a man may _____ of the bread

     b. That a man would do so and not _____ (*to be subject to eternal death*)

99. What did Jesus say that He was (**v.51**)?

_____

100. Where did Jesus say that He came from (**v.51**)?

_____

101. What did Jesus say would happen to any that ate of the living bread (**v.51**)?

_____

102. What did Jesus say the bread was that He would give (**v.51**)?

_____

---

[130] **John 6:48**: Jesus being the bread of life means *He alone has the ability to nourish a person up unto eternal life*

103. Why would He do this (*v.51*)?

_____

104. What did the Jews do, when they heard this (*v.52*)[131]?

_____

105. As they did this, what did they say (*v.52*)?

_____

106. Do you think they understood what Jesus was trying to tell them?

_____

107. What did Jesus truthfully tell the Jews they needed to eat and drink in order to have life (*eternal life*) in them (*v.53*)[132]?

        a. They needed to eat Jesus' _____

        b. They needed to drink Jesus' _____

108. Who did Jesus say has eternal life (*v.54*)?

        a. Whoever eats His _____

        b. Whoever drinks His _____

109. What did Jesus say He would do for such a person (*v.54*)?

_____

110. What did Jesus say about His flesh (*v.55*)[133]?

_____

111. What did He say about His blood (*v.55*)[134]?

_____

112. What did Jesus also say happens to those that eat His flesh and drink his blood (*v.56*)?

        a. They _____ (*to be knit together in spirit*) in Him

        b. He _____ (*to be knit together in spirit*) in them

113. What special trait does the Father that sent Jesus have (*v.57*)[135]?

_____

---

[131] **John 6:52**: Strove means *to quarrel*

[132] **John 6:53**: To eat Jesus' flesh and drink His blood speaks figuratively of the realization and belief a person must come to regarding the saving purpose of Jesus' death on the cross

[133] **John 6:55**: This meat is *food that nourishes a soul unto life eternal* (cf. **John 6:27**)

[134] **John 6:55b**: Jesus' flesh and blood being meat and drink indeed means *they are truly able to nourish those that partake unto life eternal*

[135] **John 6:57**: To be living means *to be living in an absolute sense* (which is unlimited, unconditional, and complete)

114. What special trait did the Father give to the Son (*v.57*)?

_____

115. What special thing happens to those that eat Jesus (*His flesh and blood*) (*v.57*)?

_____

116. Where did the bread that Jesus spoke of come from (*v.58*)?

_____

117. What happened to the Jews' fathers that ate the manna (*v.58*)?

_____

118. What happens to those that eat of the bread Jesus spoke of (*v.58*)?

_____

119. Where did Jesus say these words (*v.59*)?

_____

120. In what city did Jesus teach these things (*v.59*)?

_____

121. What did many of Jesus' disciples say, when they heard His words (*v.60*)?

    a. "This is a _____ (*offensive*) saying…"

    b. "Who can _____ (*to hearken to*) it?"

122. What did Jesus know that His disciples were doing (*v.61*)?

_____

123. What did He ask them (*v.61*)[136]?

_____

124. What did Jesus say might change their minds (*v.62*)?

_____

125. What did He say it was that quickened (*to make one spiritually alive*) a man (*v.63*)?

_____

126. What did He say the flesh did to profit (*to be useful to*) a man (*v.63*)?

_____

127. What did Jesus say the words He spoke to the Jews were (*v.63*)?

    a. They were _____

    b. They were _____

_____

[136] *John 6:61*: To offend means *to cause someone to distrust one that he ought to trust and obey*

128. When Jesus spoke of eating His flesh and drinking His blood, was He speaking of doing so literally or spiritually (*v.63*)?

_____

129. What did He say about some of those that heard Him (*v.64*)?

_____

130. What did Jesus know from the beginning (*the beginning of the time He gathered disciples*) (*v.64*)?

     a. Who they were that did not _____ in Him

     b. Who they were that would _____ Him

131. Because some of His disciples did not believe Him, who did Jesus say could come to Him (*v.65*)?

_____

132. From that time, what happened to Jesus' disciples (*v.66*)?

     a. Many of them went _____ (*to leave from following*)

     b. Many of them _____ no more (*to cease to be one's companion and follower*) with Him

133. What did Jesus then say to the twelve disciples (*v.67*)?

_____

134. Who spoke up with an answer (*v.68*)?

_____

135. What did this man say (*v.68-69*)?

     a. "Lord, to whom shall we _____?"

     b. "You have (*to possess*) the _____ of eternal life."

     c. "We _____ that you are that Christ (*the Messiah*)..." (*v.69*)

     d. "We are _____ (*to know*) that you are that Christ..."

136. Who else did Peter say that the Christ was (*v.69*)?

_____

137. What was Jesus' response to Peter's profession of faith (*v.70*)?

_____

138. Though Jesus chose them, what did He say one of them was (*v.70*)[137]?

_____

139. Who was Jesus talking about (*v.71*)?

_____

_____

[137] *John 6:70*: Being a devil means *that one of Jesus' disciples was acting the part of the devil or siding with him*

140. What would this man do to Jesus (*v.71*)?

_____

141. What position did this man hold (*v.71*)?

_____

142. Do you think it is best to trust in Jesus, even though we may not understand His words?

_____

143. Why should we do this (*v.68-69*)?

_____

Meditation (What God Spoke to Me About):

_____

_____

_____

_____

_____

_____

_____

_____

Application (How I Can Apply What I Learned):

_____

_____

_____

_____

_____

_____

_____

_____

Memorization (How I Can Retain What I Read):

Suggestions: *John 6:9-12; 6:26-29; 6:32-33; 6:35; 6:47-48; 6:61-69*

_____

_____

_____

Assessment (How I Am Doing With My Application and Memorization):

_____

_____

_____

_____

_____

_____

Bible Study Questions (*John 7:1-53*)

Instructions: Pray that God will help you to understand this passage. Read through this Bible passage twice: once for reading and another time for understanding. After reading, consider and answer the questions listed below. Write down notes regarding anything else God spoke to you about.

1. After the events of the previous chapter, where did Jesus choose to walk (*v.1*)?

_____

2. Where did He refuse to walk (*v.1*)[138]?

_____

3. Why did He choose not to walk there (*v.1*)?

_____

4. What special event was at hand (*v.2*)[139]?

_____

5. What did Jesus' brethren (*siblings*) say to Him, because the feast was near (*v.3*)?

    a. "_____ from here…"

    b. "Go into _____…"

6. Why did they say that Jesus should do this (*v.3*)?

_____

7. Why did they say He needed to show His works openly (*v.4*)?

    a. Because there was no one that did anything in _____

    b. Because those that do miraculous works seek (*to desire*) to be _____

    openly (*before the public*)

8. If Jesus claimed to do miraculous works, what did his siblings tell Him to do (*v.4*)?

_____

9. Why did Jesus' brethren tell Him these things (*v.5*)?

_____

10. Though there were witnesses, did they believe Jesus performed these miracles? (*v.5*)?

_____

_____

[138] *John 7:1*: Jewry was another name for Judaea (referring to the southern portion of Israel that held Jerusalem)
[139] *John 7:2*: The Feast of Tabernacles is an annual, seven day observance that occurs in October as a memorial to Israel's journey through the wilderness to the Promised Land, where they dwelled in tents

11. What was Jesus' response (*v.6*)?

      a. "My _____ (*the time appointed by God for appearing in public*) is not

      yet come…"

      b. "Your _____ is always ready."

12. What did Jesus say His siblings' relationships were with the world (*the ungodly multitude that is naturally hostile to the cause of Christ*) (*v.7*)?

_____

13. What did Jesus say His relationship was with the world (*v.7*)?

_____

14. Why did the world feel this way about Jesus (*v.7*)?

_____

15. What was Jesus' message to the world (*v.7*)?

_____

16. Do you think that people like to hear that what they do is evil?

_____

17. What did Jesus tell his brethren to do (*v.8*)?

_____

18. What did He say that He would not do yet (*v.8*)?

_____

19. Why did He say this (*v.8*)?

_____

20. After Jesus said this, what did He do (*v.9*)[140]?

_____

21. What did He decide to do, after His brethren had left for the feast (*v.10*)?

_____

22. Did Jesus go openly or in secret (*privately*) (*v.10*)?

_____

23. Who sought for Jesus at the feast (*v.11*)?

_____

24. What did these people say (*v.11*)?

_____

_____

[140] **John 7:9**: To abide means *to dwell*

25. What was there much of among the people regarding Jesus (**v.12**)[141]?

_____

26. What were the people saying about Him (**v.12**)?

     a. Some said, "He is a _____ man."

     b. Others said, "No, but He _____ (*to lead into error*) the people."

27. Who spoke openly (*publicly*) about Jesus (**v.13**)?

_____

28. Why did they not do this (**v.13**)?

_____

29. What did Jesus do when the feast was about half over (**v.14**)?

     a. He went up into the _____

     b. He _____ (*to hold discourse in order to instruct*)

30. What were the Jews' responses to Jesus' teaching (**v.15**)?

_____

31. What did they say about His teaching (**v.15**)[142]?

_____

32. What did Jesus state in response to the Jews' reactions (**v.16**)?

     a. "My _____ (*beliefs and teachings*) is not mine…"

     b. "My _____ is His that sent me."

33. What would a person know, if they did God's will (*desires*) (**v.17**)?

_____

34. What would they know about it (**v.17**)?

     a. If it be of _____

     b. If Jesus spoke of _____

35. Does Jesus' doctrine come from God or mankind (**v.16**)?

_____

36. What is true about a person that speaks of himself (*to speak from one's own mind*) (**v.18**)?

_____

---

[141] **John 7:12**: To murmur means *to have a secret debate* (in this case: about Jesus)

[142] **John 7:15**: Letters means *letters of sacred learning*

37. What is true about the person that seeks to glorify the one that sent Him (*to promote the glory of God*) (*v.18*)[143]?

       a. He is _____

       b. No _____ (*unrighteousness by which others are deceived*)

       is in Him

38. Who gave the Jews the Law (*v.19*)?

_____

39. Did any of the Jews keep (*to meet the demands of*) the Law (*v.19*)?

_____

40. What did Jesus say that the Jews wanted to do to Him (*v.19*)?

_____

41. What did the Jews say that Jesus had in response to His accusation (*v.20*)[144]?

_____

42. What did they deny that they wanted to do to Jesus (*v.20*)?

_____

43. What was Jesus' response to their denial (*v.21*)?

_____

44. What one work was Jesus referring to (*John 5:1-16*)?

_____

45. What did He say that Moses gave to them (*v.22*)[145]?

_____

46. Where did He say this practice came from (*v.22*)[146]?

_____

47. On what day did Jesus say the Jews circumcised a man (*v.22*)?

_____

48. Why would they circumcise a man on this day (*v.23*)?

_____

---

[143] *John 7:18*: "*He that seeketh his own glory that sent him*" means "*He that seeks to promote the glory of God.*"
[144] *John 7:20*: To have a devil means *to speak as though one were insane* (normally associated with possession)
[145] *John 7:22*: Jesus spoke of the rite of circumcision that was a sign of the Jews' separation from the world and commanded by the Mosaic Law (*Leviticus 12:3*), but began with Abraham (*Genesis 17:10*)
[146] *John 7:22b*: The fathers means *the ancestors of the Jews*

49. Why were the Jews angry at Jesus (*v.23*)?

_____

50. Should the Jews have been angry with Jesus for this?

_____

51. How did Jesus tell the Jews to judge (*to pronounce judgment upon the deeds of others*) (*v.24*)?

      a. To not judge according to _____ (*the outward appearance*)

      b. To judge _____ (*just*) judgment

52. What did some of the Jews ask each other about Jesus (*v.25*)?

_____

53. How did they say that Jesus spoke to them (*v.26*)?

_____

54. What was their response to Him (*v.26*)?

_____

55. What did they speculate the rulers knew about Jesus (*v.26*)?

_____

56. What did the Jews think they knew about Jesus (*v.27*)[147]?

_____

57. What did they say about Christ (*v.27*)?

_____

58. What did Jesus do as He taught in the Temple (*v.28*)[148]?

_____

59. What did He say (*v.28*)?

      a. "You all both _____ Me…"

      b. "You all _____ from where I am…"

      c. "I am not _____ (*to come before the public*) of Myself…"

      d. "He that sent Me is _____…"

60. What did Jesus say about the Jews' relationship with God (*v.28*)?

_____

61. What did Jesus say about His own relationship with God (*v.29*)?

_____

---

[147] **John 7:27**: From whence He is means *from where He came from*
[148] **John 7:28**: To cry means *to call with a loud voice*

62. Why was this true (*v.29*)?

       a. Because He was _____ (*to originate from*) Him

       b. Because He had _____ Him

63. What did the Jews seek to do to Jesus in response (*v.30*)[149]?

_____

64. What happened to Jesus (*v.30*)?

_____

65. Why did this happen (*v.30*)?

_____

66. What else happened among the Jews (*v.31*)?

_____

67. What was their reason for their decision (*v.31*)?

_____

68. Who heard that some of the Jews believed on Jesus (*v.32*)?

_____

69. Who started to take action against Jesus (*v.32*)?

       a. The _____

       b. The chief _____

70. What did they do (*v.32*)?

_____

71. How long did Jesus say that He would be with the people (*v.33*)?

_____

72. What would happen after this (*v.33*)?

_____

73. What did Jesus say the Jews would do (*v.34*)?

       a. They would _____ Him

       b. They would not _____ Him

74. What did He say about the place He was going to (*v.34*)?

_____

---

[149] *John 7:30*: To take means *to apprehend in order to imprison*

75. What was the Jews' responses to Jesus' statement (**v.35**)?

      a. "Where will He go, that we cannot _____ Him?"

      b. "Will He go to the _____ (*the dispersed Jews*) among the Gentiles?"

      c. "Will He _____ the Gentiles (*people that are not Jewish*)?"

76. What statements of Christ confused the Jews (**v.36**)?

      a. "You all shall _____ me..."

      b. "You all shall not _____ me..."

      c. "Where I am, there you all cannot _____."

77. Was Jesus speaking of going to another place on Earth or Heaven (**John 3:13**)?

_____

78. What happened on the last, great day of the feast (**v.37**)?

_____

79. What did Jesus say that any man that thirsted (*to long for those things by which the soul is refreshed and strengthened*) could do (**v.37**)?

      a. They could _____ to Him

      b. They could _____ (*to receive into the soul what serves to refresh, strengthen, and nourish it unto eternal life*)

80. What did He say would happen to those that believed on Him (**v.38**)[150]?

_____

81. Was Jesus speaking of physical or spiritual water (**v.39**)?

_____

82. Who would those that believed on Jesus receive (*to obtain*) (**v.39**)[151]?

_____

83. What was true about the Holy Ghost (**v.39**)?

_____

84. Why had this not happened yet (**v.39**)[152]?

_____

---

[150] *John 7:38* (lit): "**Out of the innermost part of a man, which is his seat of thought, will flow an abundance of that which will satisfy the needs and desires of the soul.**"

[151] *John 7:39*: Should receive means *to obtain at a set time in the future*

[152] *John 7:39b*: To be glorified means *to be restored to a state of glory in Heaven* (speaking of Jesus)

85. What different things did the Jews say about Jesus, when they heard His words (**v.40-41**)?

    a. "Of a truth, this is the _____ (*the prophet that would arise*

    before the Messiah' advent)…"

    b. "This is the _____ (*Messiah and Savior from sin*)…"

    c. "Shall _____ come out of Galilee?" (**v.41**)

86. Where did they say the scriptures stated that Christ would come from (**v.42**)[153]?

    a. He would come out of the seed (*family line*) of _____

    b. He would come out of the town of _____

87. Who also came from this town (**v.42**)?

_____

88. What was created among the people, because of Jesus (**v.43**)?

_____

89. What would some of them have done to Jesus (**v.44**)[154]?

_____

90. What happened instead (**v.44**)?

_____

91. Who did the officers (*the servants of the Sanhedrin*) report back to (**v.45**)?

    a. The chief _____

    b. The _____

92. What did these people ask the officers (**v.45**)?

_____

93. Why did they not arrest Jesus (**v.46**)?

_____

94. What questions did the religious leaders give to the officers (**v.47-48**)?

    a. "Are you all also _____ (*to be led in error*)?"

    b. "Have any of the rulers (*members of the Sanhedrin*) _____ on

    Him?" (**v.48**)

    c. "Have any of the Pharisees _____ on Him?"

---

[153] **John 7:42**: cf. **I Chronicles 17:7-14; Micah 5:2**
[154] **John 7:44**: To take means *to apprehend in order to imprison*

95. What did they say about the people who heard Jesus (**v.49**)?

     a. They did not _____ the Law

     b. They were _____ (*to be exposed to divine vengeance*)

96. Who spoke up to the religious leaders (**v.50**)?

_____

97. What had this man done previously (**v.50**)[155]?

_____

98. What relationship did this man have with the Pharisees (**v.50**)?

_____

99. What did he ask the Pharisees regarding their law (**v.51**)?

     a. "Does our law judge any man, before it _____ him?"

     b. "Does our law judge any man, before it _____ what he does?"

100. What was the reply of the religious leaders (**v.52**)?

_____

101. What did they tell him to do in regards to the scriptures (**v.52**)?

     a. To _____ (*to examine into*)

     b. To _____ (*to behold*)

102. Why did they tell him to do this (**v.52**)?

_____

103. What happened after this conversation (**v.53**)?

_____

---

[155] **John 7:50**: cf. **John 3:1-21**

Meditation (What God Spoke to Me About):

_____

_____

_____

_____

_____

_____

_____

_____

Application (How I Can Apply What I Learned):

_____

_____

_____

_____

_____

_____

_____

_____

Memorization (How I Can Retain What I Read):

Suggestions: *John 7:6-7; 7:16-19; 7:37-38*

_____

_____

_____

_____

Assessment (How I Am Doing With My Application and Memorization):

_____

_____

_____

_____

_____

_____

Bible Study Questions (*John 8:1-59*)

Instructions: Pray that God will help you to understand this passage. Read through this Bible passage twice: once for reading and another time for understanding. After reading, consider and answer the questions listed below. Write down notes regarding anything else God spoke to you about.

1. Where did Jesus go to (*v.1*)?

_____

2. Where did He go to, early in the morning (*v.2*)?

_____

3. Who came unto Him (*v.2*)?

_____

4. What He do with them (*v.2*)?

    a. He _____ down

    b. He _____ them

5. Who also came to Jesus (*v.3*)?

    a. The _____

    b. The _____

6. Who did they bring (*to lead by laying ahold of*) to Him (*v.3*)[156]?

_____

7. What did they do with her (*v.3*)[157]?

_____

8. What title did they address Jesus with (*v.4*)?

_____

9. What did they say had happened to this woman (*v.4*)?

_____

10. Who did the religious leaders say commanded them (*v.5*)?

_____

11. Where did this man command them from (*v.5*)?

_____

---

[156] **John 8:3**: To be taken means *to catch* (in this case: in the act of adultery)
[157] **John 8:3b**: To set means *to bid to stand by* (in this case: in the midst of the assembly)

12. What was the command regarding this situation (**v.5**)[158]?

_____

13. What did the religious leaders ask Jesus (**v.5**)?

_____

14. Why did they ask Jesus this (**v.6**)?

    a. They said this _____ (*to maliciously test*) Him

    b. They said this that they might have to _____ (*to accuse before*

    a judge) Him

15. What did Jesus do in response (**v.6**)?

    a. He _____ down

    b. He _____ on the ground with His finger

16. What did Jesus act like (**v.6**)?

_____

17. What did the religious leaders do in response (**v.7**)?

_____

18. What did Jesus then do (**v.7**)?

_____

19. What did He tell them (**v.7**)?

_____

20. What did Jesus turn again to do (**v.8**)?

    a. He _____ down

    b. He _____ on the ground

21. What happened to the religious leaders that heard it (**v.9**)?

    a. They were _____ (*to feel shame, because of a personal sin*)

    by their own conscience

    b. They went _____ one by one

22. How did these men leave (**v.9**)?

_____

23. Who was left, after the religious leaders left (**v.9**)?

    a. _____ was left alone

    b. The _____ was standing in the midst

_____

[158] **John 8:5**: To be stoned means *to be killed by stoning*

24. What did Jesus then do (**v.10**)?

      a. He _____ Himself up

      b. He _____ none but the woman

25. What did He ask the woman (**v.10**)?

      a. "Where are your _____?"

      b. "Has no man _____ (*to judge one to be worthy of*

      punishment) you?"

26. What was her answer (**v.11**)?

_____

27. What did Jesus then say to her (**v.11**)?

      a. "Neither do I _____ you…"

      b. "Go and _____ no more."

28. What did Jesus then say again to the Jews about Himself (**v.12**)?

_____

29. What did He say would happen to those that followed Him (*to join Him as a disciple*) (**v.12**)?

      a. They would not walk (*to frequent*) in _____ (*wickedness*

      and general ignorance of divine things)

      b. They would have the _____ (*the light by which true life is gained*)

      of life

30. Who replied back to Jesus (**v.13**)?

_____

31. What was their reply (**v.13**)?

      a. "You bear _____ (*to bear witness*) of yourself…"

      b. "Your _____ is not true."

32. Did Jesus reply that He bore record of Himself (**v.14**)?

_____

33. Even though He did this, what was special about it (**v.14**)?

_____

34. Why was this so (**v.14**)?

      a. Jesus knew from where He _____

      b. Jesus knew to where He would _____

35. What did the Pharisees not know about Jesus, in contrast (*v.14*)?

       a. They did not know from where He _____

       b. They did not know to where He would _____

36. How did Jesus say the Pharisees judged (*v.15*)[159]?

_____

37. How did Jesus say that He judged (*v.15*)[160]?

_____

38. What would have been special about Jesus judgment, if He did it (*v.16*)?

_____

39. Why was this true (*v.16*)[161]?

_____

40. Who did Jesus say was with Him and helped Him to judge (*v.16*)?

_____

41. What did He then say was written in the Jews' law (*v.17*)?

_____

42. What did He tell the Jews regarding Himself (*v.18*)?

       a. He was one that bore _____ of Himself

       b. His _____ that sent Him also bore witness of Him

43. What was the Jews' reply to Jesus' statements (*v.19*)?

_____

44. How did Jesus answer (*v.19*)?

_____

45. What did He say would have happened to them, if they had known Him (*v.19*)?

_____

46. Where did Jesus speak these words (*v.20*)[162]?

_____

47. Why was He there (*v.20*)?

_____

---

[159] **John 8:15**: To judge after the flesh means *the Pharisees judged Jesus according to His external appearance*

[160] **John 8:15b**: No man means *no one or nothing*

[161] **John 8:16**: To be alone means *to be forsaken or without a companion*

[162] **John 8:20**: The treasury was the place in the Temple where contributions were made for the service of the Temple and the support of the poor

48. What were the Jews not able to do to Jesus (**v.20**)[163]?

_____

49. Why did this happen (**v.20**)[164]?

_____

50. What did Jesus then say again to the Jews (**v.21**)?

      a. "I go my _____ (_to go away_)..."

      b. "You all shall _____ me..."

      c. "You all shall _____ in your sins..."

      d. "Where I go, you all cannot _____."

51. What question did the Jews have in response (**v.22**)?

_____

52. Why did they ask this (**v.22**)?

_____

53. Did the Jews understand what Jesus was talking about?

_____

54. What words did Jesus have further for the Jews (**v.23**)?

      a. "You all are from _____ (_the earth_)..."

      b. "I am from _____ (_Heaven_)..."

      c. "You all are of this _____..."

      d. "I am not of this _____."

55. Because the Jews were of the earth, what had Jesus said to them (**v.24**)?

_____

56. Why else did He tell them this (**v.24**)?

_____

57. If a person does not believe that Jesus is the Messiah, what will happen to them (**v.24**)?

_____

58. What question did the Jews have in response (**v.25**)?

_____

59. What was Jesus' answer (**v.25**)?

_____

---

[163] **John 8:20b**: To lay hands upon one means _to apprehend a person in order to imprison them_
[164] **John 8:20c**: The hour refers to _the hour of death that was appointed to Christ_

60. What else did He have to say (**v.26**)?

     a. He had many things to _____ of them (*to speak to them about*)

     b. He had many things to _____ of them (*to pronounce judgment*

     upon them)

61. Why did He not do this in full (**v.26**)?

     a. He that sent Jesus was _____

     b. Jesus spoke to the world those things which He _____ of Him (*the Father*)

62. What did the Jews not understand (**v.27**)?

_____

63. What did Jesus say would happen when they lifted Him up (*speaking of Jesus' elevation on the cross*)
(**v.28**)?

     a. They would _____ that He was the Messiah

     b. They would _____ that He did nothing of Himself

64. Why did Jesus speak the things that He did (**v.28**)?

_____

65. Who did He say was with Him (**v.29**)?

_____

66. Who is the one that sent Jesus (**v.27-29**)?

_____

67. Was Jesus left alone (*forsaken*) by the Father (**v.29**)?

_____

68. Why was this the case (**v.29**)?

_____

69. As Jesus spoke these words, what happen amongst the Jews (**v.30**)[165]?

_____

70. What did He tell those that believed on Him to do (**v.31**)?

_____

71. If they did this, what would happen to them (**v.31-32**)?

     a. They would be His _____ (*learners*) indeed

     b. They would know the _____

---

[165] **John 8:30**: To believe means *to trust in Jesus Christ as the Messiah and Savior from sin*

72. What happens to those that know the truth (**v.32**)[166]?

_____

73. What was the Jews' reply (**v.33**)?

     a. "We are _____ seed (_heritage_)…"

     b. "We were never in _____ (_to be in subjection to other nations_) to

     any man…"

74. What statement did they not understand from Jesus (**v.33**)?

_____

75. What did Jesus say in truth regarding those that commit sin (**v.34**)?

_____

76. What else did He say about the subject (**v.35**)?

     a. "The _____ does not abide (_to remain_) in the house forever…"

     b. "The Son _____ (_to remain_) forever

77. Because of this, if Jesus makes a person free from sin, what happens to them (**v.36**)?

_____

78. What did Jesus know about the Jews (**v.37**)?

     a. That they were of _____ seed (_heritage_)

     b. That they sought to _____ Him

79. Why did they seek to do this (**v.37**)?

_____

80. What did Jesus say He spoke of (**v.38**)?

_____

81. What did He say the Jews did (**v.38**)?

_____

82. Who did the Jews say was their father (**v.39**)?

_____

83. What did Jesus say would happen, if the Jews were this man's children (**v.39**)?

_____

84. What did the Jews want to do to Jesus (**v.40**)?

_____

_____

[166] **_John 8:32_**: To be made free means _to be set at liberty from the bondage and dominion of sin_

85. Why did they want to do this (**v.40**)?

_____

86. Where did Jesus hear the words that He gave the Jews (**v.40**)?

_____

87. Should we want to harm people for giving us the truth?

_____

88. Were the works of the Jews the works of Abraham (**v.40**)?

_____

89. Who did Jesus say the Jews did the deeds of (**v.41**)?

_____

90. What was the Jews' reply (**v.41**)[167]?

      a. "We are not born of _____..."

      b. "We have one _____, even God."

91. What did Jesus say would happen if God was their Father (**v.42**)?

_____

92. Why would this happen (**v.42**)?

      a. Because Jesus _____ forth from Him (_to leave His place with God in Heaven_)

      b. Because Jesus _____ (_to have arrived_) from Him

93. Did Jesus come to Earth on His own or did God send Him (**v.42**)?

_____

94. What did the Jews not understand about Jesus (**v.43**)[168]?

_____

95. Why did were the Jews not able to do this (**v.43**)[169]?

_____

96. Who did Jesus say the Jews' father was (**v.44**)?

_____

97. Because of this, what did He say the Jews would do (**v.44**)[170]?

_____

_____

[167] **_John 8:41_** (lit.): Then they said to Him, "**_We are not of a people given to idolatry; we have one Father: God._**"
[168] **_John 8:43_**: Jesus' speech speaks of _speech which disclosed His native country, which is Heaven_
[169] **_John 8:43b_**: To hear means _to give ear to_ (to be willing to listen to)
[170] **_John 8:44_**: To do the lusts of their father means _to do the desires of their father_ (the Devil)

98. What did Jesus say the Devil was from the beginning (*the beginning of all things*) (**v.44**)?

_____

99. What else did the Devil do (**v.44**)?

_____

100. Why did he not do this (**v.44**)?

_____

101. What happens when the Devil speaks a lie (**v.44**)[171] [172]?

_____

102. Why does this happen (**v.44**)?

    a. The Devil is a _____

    b. The Devil is the _____ of lies

103. Why did the Jews not believe Jesus' words (**v.45**)?

_____

104. Were there any that could prove that Jesus' words were sin (**v.46**)?

_____

105. If Jesus only told them the truth, what was the problem with the Jews (**v.46**)?

_____

106. What is true of those that are of God (**v.47**)[173]?

_____

107. What is true of those that are not of God (**v.47**)?

_____

108. Did the Jews believe God's words or not (**v.47**)?

_____

109. Were the Jews of God or not (**v.47**)?

_____

110. Who did the Jews truly have as their father (**v.44**)?

_____

111. What did the Jews then accuse Jesus of (**v.48**)?

    a. Being a _____ (*one that is half-Jew and half-Gentile*)

    b. Having a _____ (*to be possessed by an evil spirit*)

---

[171] **John 8:44b**: To speak means *to utter words in accordance with one's inner character*
[172] **John 8:44c**: Satan speaking lies that are of his own means that *when he speaks lies, he reveals what he truly is*
[173] **John 8:47**: To hear means *to hear with the intention of responding to the words heard*

112. What was Jesus' reply (**v.49-50**)?

       a. "I do not have a _____..."

       b. "I _____ (*to revere*) my Father..."

       c. "You all do _____ (*to insult*) me."

       d. "I seek not my own _____..." (**v.50**)

       e. "There is one that _____ (*to seek to promote the glory of God*) and

       _____ (*to judge between the righteousness and unrighteousness*

      of men)

113. What did Jesus say would happen, if a person kept (*to keep religiously*) His saying (**v.51**)[174]?

_____

114. What did the Jews again state about Jesus (**v.52**)?

_____

115. Why did they believe this about Him (**v.52**)?

       a. They thought _____ was dead

       b. They thought the _____ were dead

116. What saying of Jesus' did they think was false (**v.52**)?

_____

117. What did the Jews in turn ask Jesus (**v.53**)?

       a. "Are you _____ than our father Abraham?"

       b. "Are you _____ than the prophets?"

       c. "Who do you _____ yourself to be?"

118. Is Jesus greater than Abraham or the prophets?

_____

119. Again, what did the Jews believe about Abraham and the prophets (**v.53**)?

_____

120. How did Jesus reply regarding His honor (**v.54**)?

_____

121. Who did He say honored Him (**v.54**)?

_____

122. Who did the Jews claim the Father was to them (**v.54**)?

_____

_____

[174] **John 8:51**: To never see death means *to never experience eternal death in Hell*

123. If they claimed this and He honored Jesus, should they have believed in Him?

_____

124. What did Jesus say the Jews' relationship with the Father was (*v.55*)?

_____

125. What did Jesus say that His relationship with God was (*v.55*)?

_____

126. What would happen if Jesus denied knowing the Father (*v.55*)?

_____

127. Instead of doing this, what did He confess about God (*v.55*)?

    a. That He _____ the Father

    b. That He _____ His saying (*instruction*)

128. What did Jesus say about Abraham (*v.56*)?

    a. That he _____ to see Jesus' day (*the time when the Messiah*

    should appear before men)

    b. That he _____ Jesus' day

    c. That he was _____ when he did

129. Was Abraham on Earth when he saw Jesus' day or in Heaven?

_____

130. What was the Jews' reply (*v.57*)?

    a. "You are not yet _____ years old…"

    b. "Have you seen _____?"

131. How did Jesus answer their disbelief (*v.58*)[175]?

_____

132. What did the Jews do in reply (*v.59*)?

_____

---

[175] **John 8:58**: The proclamation of the I AM (cf. **Exodus 3:14**) was Jesus proclaiming His deity, which also proclaimed His eternality (existing before Abraham) and equality with God

133. What did Jesus do (*v.59*)?

      a. He _____ Himself (*to depart secretly*)

      b. He went out of the _____

134. How did Jesus leave this place (*v.59*)?

      a. He went through the _____ (*the middle*) of them

      b. He _____ by them (*to depart from them*)

Meditation (What God Spoke to Me About):

_____
_____
_____
_____
_____
_____
_____

Application (How I Can Apply What I Learned):

_____
_____
_____
_____
_____
_____
_____
_____

Memorization (How I Can Retain What I Read):

Suggestions: *John 8:7-11; 8:12; 8:15-16; 8:23-24; 8:31-32; 8:42-44; 8:54-59*

_____
_____
_____

Assessment (How I Am Doing With My Application and Memorization):

_____
_____
_____
_____
_____
_____
_____

Bible Study Questions (*John 9:1-41*)

Instructions: Pray that God will help you to understand this passage. Read through this Bible passage twice: once for reading and another time for understanding. After reading, consider and answer the questions listed below. Write down notes regarding anything else God spoke to you about.

1. As the chapter opens, what did Jesus do (*v.1*)[176]?

_____

2. Who did He see as He went (*v.1*)?

_____

3. How long had this man been in this condition (*v.1*)?

_____

4. What did Jesus' disciples ask Him (*v.2*)?

_____

5. Who did they think committed sin (*v.2*)?

    a. The blind _____

    b. The blind man's _____

6. Why did they think someone committed sin (*v.2*)?

_____

7. What was Jesus' answer (*v.3*)?

    a. "This man has not _____..."

    b. "His parents have not _____..."

8. Why did Jesus say this man was born blind (*v.3*)[177]?

_____

9. What did Jesus say that He had to do (*v.4*)?

_____

10. During what time would He do these things (*v.4*)[178]?

_____

11. What did Jesus say was coming (*v.4*)[179]?

_____

_____

[176] ***John 9:1***: To pass by means *to depart* (in this case: Jesus was departing the Temple (cf. ***John 8:59***))

[177] ***John 9:3***: To be made manifest means *to be made visible*

[178] ***John 9:4***: While it is still day means (lit): "***While life still gives an opportunity for me to work.***"

[179] ***John 9:4b***: The night speaks of *the time when life on Earth ceases*

12. What would happen during this time (**v.4**)?

_____

13. Do you think we should do all we can for Christ on Earth, before our time is up?

_____

14. What did Jesus say that He was, as long as He was in the world (**v.5**)?

_____

15. After He said these things, what did Jesus do (**v.6**)?

        a. He _____ on the ground

        b. He made _____ (*mud*) of the spittle

        c. He _____ (*to spread on*) the eyes of the blind man with it

16. What did Jesus then tell the blind man to do (**v.7**)?

        a. To _____

        b. To _____ in the pool of Siloam (*a fountain in Jerusalem*)

17. What does the word *Siloam* mean (**v.7**)?

_____

18. What did the blind man do (**v.7**)?

        a. He _____ his way

        b. He _____

        c. He came (*to return*) _____

19. What did the observing people say, when they saw the healed man (**v.8**)?

_____

20. Who were those that said this (**v.8**)?

        a. His _____

        b. Those that before had seen that he was _____

21. What did some of them say about him (**v.9**)?

_____

22. What did others say about him (**v.9**)?

_____

23. What did he say about himself (**v.9**)?

_____

24. Because of the man's testimony, what did the crowd ask him (**v.10**)?

_____

25. How did the healed man answer (**v.11**)?

      a. "A man named _____ made clay…"

      b. "He _____ my eyes…"

      c. "He said to me, 'Go to the pool of Siloam and _____'…"

      d. "I _____…"

      e. "I _____…"

      f. "I _____ sight."

26. What did the Jews then ask him (**v.12**)?

_____

27. What was his answer (**v.12**)?

_____

28. Who did the crowd bring the healed man to (**v.13**)?

_____

29. On what special day did Jesus heal the blind man (**v.14**)?

_____

30. What did the Pharisees ask the healed man (**v.15**)?

_____

31. What was his reply (**v.15**)?

      a. "He put _____ upon my eyes…"

      b. "I _____…"

      c. "I do _____."

32. What did some of the Pharisees say in response (**v.16**)?

_____

33. Why did they say this (**v.16**)?

_____

34. What did some of the other Pharisees say about the situation (**v.16**)?

_____

35. Because of this, what was there among the Pharisees (**v.16**)?

_____

36. What then did the Pharisees ask the healed man of Jesus (**v.17**)?

_____

37. What was the man's reply (*v.17*)?

_____

38. Did the Jews truly believe that the man had been born blind (*v.18*)?

_____

39. Who did they call to prove his story (*v.18*)?

_____

40. What did they ask them (*v.19*)?

    a. "Is this your son, who you all say was born _____?"

    b. "How then does he now _____?"

41. What was the healed man's parents' response (*v.20-21*)?

    a. "We know that this is our _____..."

    b. "We know that he was born _____..."

    c. "By what means he now _____, we do not know..." (*v.21*)

    d. "He is of _____ (*adult age*); ask him..."

    e. "He shall _____ for himself."

42. Why did they speak these words (*v.22*)?

_____

43. What had the Jews already agreed to do regarding those that confessed Jesus as the Christ (*v.22*)[180]?

_____

44. Because of this, what did the man's parents say (*v.23*)?

_____

45. Which do you think is more important (**circle one**):   **confessing Christ**   **fearing men**

46. What was the Jews' next course of action (*v.24*)?

_____

47. What did they say to him about Jesus (*v.24*)?

    a. "Give _____ the praise..."

    b. "We know that this man is a _____."

48. What was the healed man's reply (*v.25*)?

_____

49. What was the one thing this man knew (*v.25*)?

_____

_____

[180] *John 9:22*: To be put out of the synagogue means *to be excommunicated*

50. What did the Jews then ask the healed man about Jesus (**v.26**)?

     a. "What _____ He do to you?"

     b. "How did He _____ your eyes?"

51. What was the man's reply (**v.27**)?

     a. "I have _____ you already…"

     b. "You all did not _____…"

     c. "Because of this, would you all _____ it again?"

     d. "Will you all also be His _____?"

52. What did the Jews then do to the healed man (**v.28**)[181]?

_____

53. What did they say to him (**v.28-29**)?

     a. "You are His _____ (*learner*)…"

     b. "We are Moses' _____."

     c. "We know that _____ spoke to Moses…" (**v.29**)

     d. "We do not know from _____ this fellow is."

54. How did the healed man answer them (**v.30-31**)?

     a. "Why is it a _____ (*surprising*) thing that you all do not know

     from where He is?"

     b. "Yet He has _____ my eyes."

     c. "We know that God does not hear _____." (**v.31**)

55. Whose prayers did the healed man say that God heard (**v.31**)?

     a. Any that are _____ of God

     b. Any that do God's _____ (*desires*)

56. What did the man say had not happened since the world began (**v.32**)?

_____

57. What did he say about Jesus (**v.33**)?

_____

58. What was the Jews' answer (**v.34**)?

     a. "You were altogether born in _____…"

     b. "Do you now _____ us?"

---

[181] **John 9:28**: To revile means *to heap abuse upon* (primarily verbal abuse)

59. What did they do to the healed man (**v.34**)?

_____

60. What did Jesus hear about the healed man (**v.35**)?

_____

61. What did He do in response (**v.35**)?

_____

62. What did He ask the healed man, when He had done so (**v.35**)?

_____

63. What was the healed man's reply (**v.36**)?

_____

64. How did Jesus answer him (**v.37**)?

       a. "You have _____ Him…"

       b. "It is He that _____ with you."

65. How did the healed man reply (**v.38**)?

_____

66. What did he do (**v.38**)?

_____

67. Why did Jesus say that He came into the world (**v.39**)?

_____

68. What would be the results of this action (**v.39**)[182]?

       a. Those that saw would not _____

       b. Those that saw would be made _____

69. Who were some that were with Jesus and heard these words (**v.40**)?

_____

70. What did they ask Him (**v.40**)?

_____

71. What did Jesus say would happen to them, if they were blind (**v.41**)?

_____

72. What did He say happened to them, because they professed to see (**v.41**)?

_____

_____

[182] **John 9:39**: The blindness Jesus speaks of is *spiritual blindness*

73. Though most Pharisees professed to be sinless, were they sinless (*Romans 3:23*)?

_____

74. If some Pharisees saw the truth of their sin, what else could they see (*v.35-37*)?

_____

Meditation (What God Spoke to Me About):

_____
_____
_____
_____
_____
_____
_____
_____

Application (How I Can Apply What I Learned):

_____
_____
_____
_____
_____
_____
_____
_____

Memorization (How I Can Retain What I Read):

Suggestions: *John 9:1-5; 9:24-25; 9:35-38*

_____
_____
_____

Assessment (How I Am Doing With My Application and Memorization):

_____
_____
_____
_____
_____
_____

Bible Study Questions (*John 10:1-42*)

Instructions: Pray that God will help you to understand this passage. Read through this Bible passage twice: once for reading and another time for understanding. After reading, consider and answer the questions listed below. Write down notes regarding anything else God spoke to you about.

1. As Jesus continues to speak (from **John 9**), who does he say is a thief and a robber (**v.1**)?

_____

2. Who is he that enters into the sheepfold by the door (**v.2**)?

_____

3. What does the porter (*the doorkeeper*) do, when this person comes (**v.3**)?

_____

4. What do the sheep do, when this person comes (**v.3**)?

_____

5. What does this person do with the sheep (**v.3**)?

     a. He _____ his own sheep by name

     b. He _____ them out

6. What happens, when he puts forth (*to let the sheep out of the fold*) his own sheep (**v.4**)?

     a. He goes _____ them

     b. The sheep _____ him

7. Why do the sheep do this (**v.4**)?

_____

8. What will the sheep do if a stranger comes (**v.5**)?

     a. They will not _____

     b. They will _____ from him

9. Why will the sheep do this (**v.5**)?

_____

10. What special type of story was Jesus giving (**v.6**)[183]?

_____

11. Did the people understand what Jesus was speaking to them (**v.6**)?

_____

12. Who did Jesus say that He was (**v.7**)?

_____

_____

[183] **John 10:6**: A parable is *an earthly story with a heavenly meaning*

13. Who were all that ever came before Jesus (**v.8**)?

_____

14. What happened, when these people came (**v.8**)?

_____

15. Who did Jesus say again that He was (**v.9**)?

_____

16. What did He say would happen, if any person entered in by Him (**v.9**)?

    a. They would be _____ (*to be saved from the penalty of sin*)

    b. They would go _____ and _____ (*to enter and exit the fold as*

    the Savior allows and guides)

    c. They would find _____ (*to never lack the supply needed for*

    true life)

17. Why does the thief come to the sheepfold (**v.10**)?

    a. To _____

    b. To _____ (*to slaughter*)

    c. To _____ (*to kill*)

18. Why did Jesus come to the sheepfold (**v.10**)?

    a. That they might have _____

    b. That they might have it more _____

19. Who else did Jesus state that He was (**v.11**)?

_____

20. What did He say He would do for the sheep (**v.11**)?

_____

21. What did Jesus have to say about the hireling (*one hired*) (**v.12**)?

    a. He is not the _____

    b. He does not own the _____

22. What did He say the hireling would do, when he saw the wolf coming (**v.12**)?

    a. He _____ (*to wrongfully desert*) the sheep

    b. He _____ (*to seek safety by flight*)

23. What then happens to the sheep (**v.12**)?

    a. The wolf _____ (*to seize and carry off by force*) them

    b. The wolf _____ them

24. Why did Jesus say the hireling would flee from the wolf (**v.13**)?

    a. Because he is a _____ (*one hired*)

    b. Because he does not _____ (*to care about*) for the sheep

25. Who did Jesus again say that He was (**v.14**)?

_____

26. Because He has this position, what is true about Him (**v.14**)?

    a. He _____ His sheep

    b. He is _____ of His sheep

27. Who else did Jesus say knew Him (**v.15**)?

_____

28. Because He knew Him, who did Jesus know (**v.15**)?

_____

29. Again, what did Jesus say that He would do for the sheep (**v.15**)?

_____

30. What else did Jesus say that He had (**v.16**)?

_____

31. What did He say would happen to these sheep (**v.16**)?

    a. He would _____ (*to lead and guide*) them

    b. They would _____ His voice

32. Once this happens, how many sheepfolds did Jesus say there would be (**v.16**)?

_____

33. How many shepherds are there to lead the sheep (**v.16**)?

_____

34. Why did Jesus say that the Father loved Him (**v.17**)[184]?

_____

35. Who would take Jesus' life from Him (**v.18**)?

_____

36. Why is this the case (**v.18**)?

_____

---

[184] **John 10:17**: To take means *to receive* (in this case: Jesus would receive His life back again)

37. What did Jesus say that He had the power (*to have the power of choice*) to do (**v.18**)?

     a. To _____ down His life

     b. To _____ (*to receive*) His life again

38. Who did Jesus receive this command from (**v.18**)?

_____

39. With these things being true, did Jesus give Himself for our sins or was He murdered (**v.17-18**)?

_____

40. What was there among the Jews, because of Jesus' sayings (**v.19**)?

_____

41. What did many of them say about Jesus (**v.20**)?

     a. "He has a _____ (*a demon or evil spirit*)..."

     b. "He is _____ (*to not be in one's right mind*)."

     c. "Why do you all _____ (*to listen to*) Him?"

42. What did others say about Him (**v.21**)?

_____

43. What question did they ask the disbelieving Jews (**v.21**)?

_____

44. What special event was now occurring at Jerusalem (**v.22**)[185]?

_____

45. At what time of year did this take place (**v.22**)?

_____

46. To where did Jesus walk in the Temple (**v.23**)[186]?

_____

47. Who gathered around Him (**v.24**)?

_____

48. What did they ask Him (**v.24**)[187]?

_____

_____

[185] **John 10:22**: The Feast of the Dedication was a fairly recent annual event that was instituted by Judas Maccabaeus in 164BC to memorialize the cleansing of the Temple from the pollution of Antiochus Epiphanes. This was an eight day event that would occur in the middle of our December (beginning the 25th of Chislev)

[186] **John 10:23**: Solomon's porch was a covered walkway in the Temple that survived earlier Babylonian destruction.

[187] **John 10:24**: To make us doubt means *to hold us in suspense between hope and doubt*

49. What did they demand of Him (**v.24**)[188]?

_____

50. What was Jesus' response (**v.25**)?

      a. "I _____ you…"

      b. "You all did not _____."

51. What did He say bore witness (*to testify*) of Him (**v.25**)?

_____

52. Why did He say they did not believe in Him (**v.26**)?

_____

53. Had Jesus already told them this (**v.26**)?

_____

54. What else did He tell them about His sheep (**v.27-28**)?

      a. "My sheep _____ (*to yield with obedience to*) my voice…"

      b. "I _____ them…"

      c. "They _____ me…"

      d. "I _____ to them eternal life…" (**v.28**)

      e. "They shall never _____ (*to lose eternal life*)…"

      f. "Neither shall any man _____ (*to snatch away*) them out of my hand."

55. What did Jesus say about His Father in Heaven (**v.29**)?

      a. He _____ His sheep to Him

      b. He is _____ than all

56. Who did He say would be able to pluck His sheep from His Fathers hand (**v.29**)?

_____

57. What special relationship does Jesus have with His Father (**v.30**)[189]?

_____

58. If we are Jesus' sheep, can Satan pluck us from the Father's hand (**v.29**)?

_____

59. If we are Jesus' sheep, can our sin pluck us from the Father's hand (**v.29**)?

_____

_____

[188] **John 10:24b**: Plainly means *openly or frankly*

[189] **John 10:30**: To be one means *to be equal and united* (this is a claim of Jesus' equality with God the Father)

60. Once we are Jesus' sheep, who can pluck us from the Father's hand (*v.29*)?

_____

61. What was the Jews' response to Jesus' declaration (*v.31*)?

_____

62. What did Jesus say He had showed them from His Father (*v.32*)?

_____

63. Because of this, what did He ask the Jews (*v.32*)?

_____

64. Why did the Jews say they were going to stone Jesus (*v.33*)?

    a. Not because of any _____ work

    b. Instead, because of _____ (*injurious speech against the divine*)

    c. Because, He, being a man, made Himself _____

65. Did the Jews understand that Jesus was claiming to be equal with God (*v.30-33*)?

_____

66. What did Jesus say was written in the Jews' law (*v.34*)[190]?

_____

67. Who did Jesus say wrote those words (*v.35*)?

_____

68. What did He say about the scriptures (*v.35*)[191]?

_____

69. What did Jesus say about Himself (*v.36*)[192]?

    a. He had been _____ by the Father

    b. He had been _____ into the world by the Father

70. What had the Jews said about Jesus (*v.36*)?

_____

71. Why did Jesus say that they said this (*v.36*)?

_____

72. When did He say that the Jews should not believe Him (*v.37*)?

_____

---

[190] *John 10:34*: cf. *Psalm 82:6*
[191] *John 10:35*: To not be broken means *to not be subverted or done away with* (speaking of the scriptures)
[192] *John 10:36*: To be sanctified means *to be separated by having been given the office of Messiah by the Father*

73. What did Jesus say the Jews should do, if He did the works of His Father, even though they did not believe in Him (*v.38*)?

_____

74. Why did He say they should do this (*v.38*)?

     a. That they all might _____

     b. That they all might _____ that the Father was in Him, and He

     in the Father

75. Because of Jesus' words, what did the Jews seek to do again (*v.39*)[193]?

_____

76. What happened to Jesus instead (*v.39*)?

_____

77. Where did He go (*v.40*)?

_____

78. What had happened there (*v.40*)?

_____

79. What did Jesus do there (*v.40*)[194]?

_____

80. What happened, while Jesus was there (*v.41*)[195]?

_____

81. What did they say about Jesus (*v.41*)?

     a. "John (the Baptist) did no _____..."

     b. "All the things that John spoke of this man were _____."

82. What happened as Jesus stayed at this place (*v.42*)?

_____

---

[193] **John 10:39**: To take means *to apprehend in order to imprison*
[194] **John 10:40**: To abide means *to remain*
[195] **John 10:41**: To resort means *to come*

Meditation (What God Spoke to Me About):

_____

_____

_____

_____

_____

_____

_____

Application (How I Can Apply What I Learned):

_____

_____

_____

_____

_____

_____

_____

_____

Memorization (How I Can Retain What I Read):

Suggestions: *John 10:1-5; 10:7-9; 10:11-18; 10:27-30*

_____

_____

_____

Assessment (How I Am Doing With My Application and Memorization):

_____

_____

_____

_____

_____

_____

John 1-10 Answer Key

(John 1:1-51)

1. The Word
2. a. God b. God c. Beginning, God
3. He made all things
4. No
5. Yes
6. Life
7. The light of men
8. Shone in the darkness
9. It did not comprehend it
10. A man named John
11. a. Come, witness b. Witness, Light
12. That all men through Him might believe
13. No
14. To bear witness of that Light
15. a. True b. Lights, comes
16. a. In b. Made c. Knew d. Came e. Received
17. They were given power to become the sons of God
18. a. Receive b. Believe
19. a. Blood b. Flesh c. Man d. God
20. a. Flesh b. Dwelled c. Beheld, glory d. Grace, Truth
21. The glory of the only begotten of the Father
22. a. Spoke b. Comes, preferred, before
23. a. Fullness b. Grace, grace
24. Moses
25. Grace and Truth
26. No man
27. The only begotten Son
28. He is in the bosom of the Father
29. That of John the Baptist
30. a. Priests b. Levites
31. "Who are you?"
32. "I am not the Christ."
33. a. Elias b. Prophet
34. "I am not." "No."
35. a. Who b. Say
36. So they could give an answer to those that sent them
37. "I am the voice of one crying in the wilderness."
38. "Make straight the way of the Lord."

39. Esaias
40. Pharisees
41. "Why do you baptize?"
42. Water
43. a. Stood b. Knew c. After, before d. Unloose
44. Bethabara
45. Baptizing
46. Jesus
47. "Behold, the Lamb of God..."
48. Take away the sins of the world
49. After
50. Before
51. Before
52. a. Knew b. Manifest c. Baptizing
53. a. Spirit, dove b. Spirit
54. No
55. He that sent him to baptize (God)
56. a. Descending b. Remaining
57. He would baptize with the Holy Ghost
58. That Jesus was the Son of God
59. Two of his disciples
60. "Behold, the Lamb of God!"
61. They followed Jesus
62. a. Turned b. Seek
63. "Rabbi, where do you dwell?"
64. Master
65. "Come and see."
66. a. Came b. Saw c. Abode
67. About the tenth hour
68. Andrew
69. Simon Peter
70. He first found his own brother
71. "We have found the Messiah."
72. Christ
73. He brought him to Jesus
74. a. Simon b. Cephas
75. A stone
76. Into Galilee
77. Philip
78. "Follow me."
79. In Bethsaida
80. Andrew and Peter
81. Nathanael
82. a. Moses, prophets b. Jesus, Joseph

83. "Can there any good thing come out of Nazareth?"

84. "Come and see."

85. a. Israelite b. Guile

86. "From where do you know me?"

87. a. Philip b. Fig

88. Yes

89. a. Son b. King

90. a. Fig, believe b. Greater

91. a. Heaven b. Angels

(John 2:1-25)

1. There was a marriage

2. In Cana of Galilee

3. The mother of Jesus

4. a. Jesus b. Disciples

5. Wine

6. "They have no wine."

7. a. Woman b. Hour

8. "Whatsoever He says unto you, do it."

9. Six water pots of stone

10. The purifying of the Jews

11. Two or three firkins apiece

12. "Fill the water pots with water."

13. To the brim

14. a. Draw b. Bear, governor

15. They bare it

16. Yes

17. a. Tasted b. Where c. Called

18. The servants

19. The good wine

20. That which was worse

21. The good wine

22. Jesus

23. First

24. a. Manifested b. Believed

25. Down to Capernaum

26. a. Mother b. Brethren c. Disciples

27. Not many days

28. Jerusalem

29. The Jews' Passover

30. a. Sold b. Money

31. a. Scourge b. Drove c. Drove
d. Poured e. Overthrew

32. a. Hence b. House, merchandise

33. "The zeal of your house has eaten me up."

34. A sign

35. a. Destroy b. Three

36. Forty-six years

37. No

38. His body

39. After He was risen from the dead

40. a. Remembered b. Believed

41. Many believed in His name

42. When they saw the miracles He did

43. He did not commit Himself to them

44. He knew all men

45. No

46. He knew what was in man

(John 3:1-36)

1. a. Pharisees b. Nicodemus c. Ruler

2. At night

3. Rabbi

4. That He was a teacher come from God

5. No man could do the miracles that He did, except God was with Him

6. "Except a man be born again, he cannot see the Kingdom of God."

7. They must be born again

8. a. Born b. Enter, born

9. No

10. a. Water b. Spirit

11. Flesh

12. Spirit

13. That He said unto him, "You all must be born again."

14. a. Lists b. Sound c. Comes, goes

15. The Spirit of God

16. "How can these things be?"

17. No

18. a. Master b. Know

19. a. Know b. Testify

20. They did not receive it

21. a. Earthly b. Heavenly

22. No man

23. The Son of Man (Jesus)

24. In Heaven

25. Lift up the serpent

26. He would be lifted up

27. So that whoever believed in Him would not perish, but have eternal life

28. The world

29. He sent His only begotten Son

30. That whosoever believed in Him would not perish, but have everlasting life

31. By believing in the Son (Jesus)

32. a. Condemn b. Saved

33. Through the Son (Jesus)

34. Those that believe (on the Son)

35. Those that do not believe (on the Son)

36. Because they have not believed in the name of the only begotten Son of God (Jesus)

37. a. Light b. Darkness, Light

38. Because their deeds were evil

39. a. Hate b. Come

40. Lest their deeds be reproved

41. They come to the Light

42. That their deeds may be made manifest

43. Their deeds are wrought in God

44. Into the land of Judaea

45. a. Tarried b. Baptized

46. John the Baptist

47. In Aenon, near to Salem

48. There was much water there

49. a. Came b. Baptized

50. He was not yet cast into prison

51. A question

52. Purifying

53. Rabbi

54. "He that was with you beyond Jordan."

55. He bore witness of Him

56. Baptizing

57. All men came to Him

58. We can receive nothing, except it is given to us from Heaven

59. Yes

60. a. Christ b. Before

61. The bridegroom

62. No

63. a. Stands b. Hears c. Rejoices

64. As His friend

65. The Bridegroom

66. His joy was fulfilled

67. a. Increase b. Decrease

68. He is above all

69. a. Earthly b. Speak

70. He is above all

71. a. Seen b. Heard

72. No man

73. They have set to their seal that God is true

74. He speaks the words of God

75. God does not give His Spirit by measure to Him

76. a. Loves b. Given

77. He that believes on the Son (Jesus)

78. He that does not believe the Son

79. The wrath of God abides on him

(John 4:1-54)

1. a. Made b. Baptized

2. His disciples

3. a. Judaea b. Galilee

4. He had to

5. Sychar

6. Near to the parcel of ground that Jacob gave to his son Joseph

7. Jacob's well

8. He was wearied with His journey

9. The sixth hour (noon)

10. A woman of Samaria

11. "Give me to drink."

12. They were gone to buy meat

13. The Jews have no dealings with the Samaritans

14. a. Gift b. Drink

15. Living water

16. Sir

17. a. Nothing b. Deep c. Living d. Greater

18. Yes

19. a. Gave b. Drank

20. They would thirst again

21. They would never thirst

22. A well of water

23. Spring up into everlasting life

24. Everlasting life

25. "Sir, give me this water…"

26. a. Thirst b. Draw

27. No

28. Physical living water

29. a. Go b. Husband c. Come

30. "I have no husband."

31. Yes

32. Yes

33. Five

34. No

35. "Sir, I perceive that you are a prophet."

36. In this mountain (Mount Gerizim)

37. Jerusalem

38. a. Mountain b. Jerusalem

39. The Father

40. They did not know what they worshipped

41. They knew what they worshipped

42. Salvation was of the Jews

43. a. Coming b. Was

44. True worshippers

45. a. Spirit b. Truth

46. The Father

47. A Spirit

48. a. Spirit b. Truth

49. No

50. Yes

51. The Messiah

52. Christ

53. All things

54. "I that speak unto you am He."

55. The Messiah (Christ)

56. His disciples

57. That He talked with the woman

58. a. Seek b. Talk

59. a. Left b. City

60. a. Come b. Told c. Christ

61. Yes

62. Yes

63. We should be so excited that Jesus is the Christ that we tell others about Him, so that they can believe too

64. a. Went b. Came

65. Eat

66. "I have meat to eat that you know not of."

67. "Has any man brought Him ought to eat?"

68. No

69. a. Will, sent b. Finish

70. Personal answer

71. There are yet four months and then comes the harvest

72. a. Eyes b. Look

73. Because they were white already to harvest

74. a. Wages b. Fruit

75. a. Sows b. Reaps

76. "One sows and another reaps."

77. He sent them to reap

78. Whereon they bestowed no labor

79. Other men

80. Entering into their labors

81. Neither

82. They believed on Jesus

83. Because of the saying of the woman

84. Many

85. Yes

86. Tarry with them

87. Two days

88. Many more believed in Jesus

89. Because of His own word

90. a. Saying b. Heard c. Christ

91. To be the Savior of the world

92. Galilee

93. Because a prophet has no honor in his own country

94. They received Him

95. They saw all the things He did at Jerusalem at the feast

96. They were also at the feast

97. Cana of Galilee

98. He made the water into wine

99. A certain nobleman

100. Capernaum

101. a. Went b. Besought

102. a. Come b. Heal

103. His son was at the point of death

104. Signs and wonders

105. "Sir, come down ere my child die."

106. No

107. Yes

108. To go his way

109. His child lived

110. a. Believed b. Went

111. His servants

112. His son lived

113. What hour he began to amend (heal)

114. Yesterday at the seventh hour

115. It was the same hour when Jesus said, "Your son lives."

116. He believed and his whole house

117. Second

(John 5:1-47)

1. A feast of the Jews

2. Jerusalem

3. A pool

4. Bethesda

5. Five

6. A great multitude

7. a. Impotent b. Blind c. Halt d. Withered

8. Waiting for the moving of the water

9. An angel

10. a. Season b. Troubled

11. They were made whole of whatever disease they had

12. A certain man

13. Thirty-eight years

14. Jesus

15. He knew the man had been a long time in that case

16. "Will you be made whole?"

17. No one (man)

18. Another would step down before him

19. a. Rise b. Take c. Walk

20. a. Whole b. Took c. Walked

21. Immediately

22. The Sabbath day

23. a. Sabbath b. Lawful

24. The one that made him whole

25. "What man said unto you, 'Take up your bed and walk.'?"

26. No

27. Jesus had conveyed Himself away

28. There was a multitude in that place

29. Jesus

30. In the Temple

31. a. Whole b. Sin

32. A worse thing would come to him

33. a. Departed b. Jesus

34. a. Persecute b. Slay

35. Because He did those things on the Sabbath

36. a. Works b. Work

37. To kill Him

38. a. Broken b. Father

39. He made Himself to be equal with God

40. Yes

41. a. Nothing b. Father c. Son

42. Because He loves the Son

43. Greater works than what He had already done

44. That they would marvel at them

45. a. Raises b. Quickens

46. He quickens whom He will

47. Yes

48. Yes

49. No man

50. The Son

51. That all men would honor the Son

52. God the Son

53. God the Father

54. Because the Father has sent the Son

55. a. Hear b. Believe

56. a. Condemnation b. Death, life

57. a. Dead b. Hear

58. a. Life b. Life

59. The authority to execute judgment

60. Because He is the Son of Man

61. Not to marvel

62. a. Graves b. Forth

63. The resurrection of life

64. The resurrection of damnation

65. Nothing

66. He judges

67. His judgment is just

68. a. Will b. Will

69. His witness would not be true

70. Because another bore witness of Him

71. True

72. John (the Baptist)

73. Witness unto the truth

74. No

75. What God thought of Him

76. What God thinks of us

77. That they might be saved

78. a. Light b. Light

79. They were willing to rejoice in his light for a season

80. It was a greater witness

81. a. Finish b. Works c. Witness, sent

82. God the Father

83. He sent the Son (Jesus)

84. a. Heard, voice b. Seen c. Word

85. Because they did not believe Jesus, whom the Father sent

86. Search the scriptures

87. a. Eternal life b. Testified c. Come, life

88. Men

89. God

90. They did not have the love of God in them

91. Jesus came in His Father's name and they did not receive Him

92. They would receive him

93. a. Honor b. Honor

94. Praise from God

95. He would not accuse them to the Father

96. Moses

97. They trusted him

98. They would have believed Jesus

99. Because Moses wrote of Him

100. No

101. They could not believe Jesus' words

(John 6:1-71)

1. The Sea of Galilee

2. The Sea of Tiberius

3. A great multitude

4. Because they saw the miracles He did on them that were diseased

5. A mountain

6. He sat

7. His disciples

8. Passover

9. It was a feast of the Jews

10. A great company

11. Philip

12. "Where shall we buy bread that these may eat?"

13. To prove him

14. He already knew what He would do

15. "Two hundred pennyworth of bread is not sufficient for them, that every one of them may take a little."

16. Andrew

17. Simon Peter

18. a. Lad b. Five, two c. Many

19. No

20. To make the men sit down

21. Much grass

22. They sat down

23. About five thousand

24. a. Loaves b. Thanks c. Distributed

25. They distributed to them that sat down

26. The fishes

27. As much as they would

28. Until they were filled

29. To gather the fragments that remained

30. That nothing be lost

31. a. Gathered b. Filled, five

32. He gave them over and above

33. "This is of a truth that prophet that should come into the world."

34. a. Force b. King

35. He departed again into a mountain

36. No

37. Down unto the sea

38. Even (evening)

39. a. Ship b. Sea

40. Capernaum

41. a. Dark b. Come c. Arose, wind

42. a. Walking b. Drawing

43. They were afraid

44. a. I b. Afraid

45. They willingly received Him into the ship

46. They were immediately at the land where they went

47. a. Sea b. Boats c. Boat d. Alone

48. The disciples

49. Boats

50. Tiberius

51. a. Shipping b. Capernaum

52. They were seeking for Jesus

53. On the other side of the sea

54. "Rabbi, when did you come here?"

55. a. Miracles b. Loaves c. Filled

56. a. Perishes b. Endures

57. The Son of Man

58. God the Father has sealed Him

59. To work the works of God

60. Yes

61. That they believe on Him whom the Father had sent

62. No

63. a. Sign b. Work

64. Because their fathers ate manna in the desert

65. Bread

66. Bread and fish

67. a. Moses b. Father

68. a. Heaven b. Life

69. To give them that bread

70. Yes

71. The bread of life

72. They would never hunger

73. They would never thirst

74. a. Seen b. Believe

75. All that the Father gave Him

76. He would in no wise cast out
77. a. Heaven b. Heaven
78. a. Nothing b. Raise
79. That every one that saw the Son and believed on Him would have everlasting life
80. a. See b. Believe
81. Jesus will raise them up at the last day
82. Because He said, "I am the bread which came down from Heaven."
83. a. Joseph b. Father
84. How He said, "I came down from Heaven."
85. To not murmur amongst themselves
86. No man
87. If the Father draws them
88. They will be raised up at the last day
89. "And they shall be all taught of God."
90. a. Heard b. Learned
91. No man
92. He which is of God
93. "He that believes on me has everlasting life."
94. By believing in Jesus
95. The bread of life
96. Manna
97. They were dead
98. a. Eat b. Die
99. The living bread
100. Heaven
101. They would live forever
102. His flesh
103. For the life of the world
104. They strove amongst themselves
105. "How can this man give us His flesh to eat?"
106. No
107. a. Flesh b. Blood
108. a. Flesh b. Blood
109. He would raise them up at the last day
110. It was meat indeed
111. It was drink indeed
112. a. Dwelled b. Dwelled
113. He is living
114. He is alive
115. He would live by Jesus Christ
116. Heaven
117. They died
118. They will live forever
119. In a synagogue

120. Capernaum
121. a. Hard b. Hear
122. Murmuring
123. "Does this offend you?"
124. If they saw the Son of Man ascend where He was before
125. The spirit
126. Nothing
127. a. Spirit b. Life
128. Spiritually
129. They did not believe Him
130. a. Believe b. Betray
131. No man, except it were given unto him of the Father
132. a. Back b. Walked
133. "Will you all also go away?"
134. Simon Peter
135. a. Go b. b. Words c. Believe d. Sure
136. The Son of the living God
137. "Have not I chosen you twelve...?"
138. A devil
139. Judas Iscariot, the son of Simon
140. He would betray Jesus
141. He was one of the twelve disciples
142. Yes
143. Because He is the Christ, the Son of the living God

(John 7:1-53)

1. In Galilee
2. In Jewry
3. Because the Jews sought to kill Him
4. The Feast of the Tabernacles
5. a. Depart b. Judaea
6. That His disciples may also see His works
7. a. Secret b. Known
8. To show Himself to the world
9. Because they did not believe in Him
10. No
11. a. Time b. Time
12. It could not hate them
13. It hated Him
14. Because He testified of it
15. That its deeds were evil
16. No
17. To go up to the feast
18. Go up to the feast

19. His time was not yet fully come
20. He abode still in Galilee
21. To also go up to the feast
22. In secret
23. The Jews
24. "Where is He?"
25. Murmuring
26. a. Good b. Deceives
27. No man
28. For fear of the Jews
29. a. Temple b. Taught
30. They marveled
31. "How does this man know letters; having never learned?"
32. a. Doctrine b. Doctrine
33. They would know of the doctrine
34. a. God b. Himself
35. God
36. He seeks his own glory
37. a. True b. Unrighteousness
38. Moses
39. No
40. To kill Him
41. A devil
42. To kill Him
43. "I have done one work, and you all marvel."
44. The healing of the lame man at the pool
45. Circumcision
46. Their fathers
47. The Sabbath day
48. That the Law of Moses should not be broken
49. Because He made a man whole on the Sabbath day
50. No
51. a. Appearance b. Righteous
52. "Is not this He, whom they seek to kill?"
53. Boldly
54. They said nothing to Him
55. That He was the Christ
56. From where He was come
57. That no one knew from where He was come
58. He cried
59. a. Know b. Know c. Come d. True
60. That they did not know Him
61. That He knew Him
62. a. From b. Sent

63. To take Him
64. No man laid hands on Him
65. Because His hour was not yet come
66. They believed on Him
67. They doubted that any other man would do more miracles than Jesus did
68. The Pharisees
69. a. Pharisees b. Priests
70. They sent officers to take Him
71. Yet a little while
72. He would go unto Him that sent Him
73. a. Seek b. Find
74. That where He was, they could not go
75. a. Find b. Dispersed c. Teach
76. a. Seek b. Find c. Come
77. Heaven
78. Jesus stood and cried
79. a. Come b. Drink
80. That out of his belly would flow rivers of living water
81. Spiritual water
82. The Spirit of God
83. That those that believed on Jesus would receive Him
84. Because Jesus was not yet glorified
85. a. Prophet b. Christ c. Christ
86. a. David b. Bethlehem
87. David
88. A division
89. Taken Him
90. No man laid hands on Him
91. a. Priests b. Pharisees
92. "Why have you all not brought Him?"
93. Because no man had ever spoken like Him
94. a. Deceived b. Believed c. Believed
95. a. Know b. Cursed
96. Nicodemus
97. Came to Jesus by night
98. He was one of them
99. a. Hear b. Knows
100. "Are you also of Galilee?"
101. a. Search b. Look
102. Because no prophet arose out of Galilee
103. Every man went to his own house

(John 8:1-59)

1. To the mount of Olives
2. The temple
3. All the people
4. a. Sat b. Taught
5. a. Scribes b. Pharisees
6. A woman taken in adultery
7. They set her in the midst
8. Master
9. She was taken in the very act of adultery
10. Moses
11. The law
12. That the woman should be stoned
13. "What do you say?"
14. a. Tempting b. Accuse
15. a. Stooped b. Wrote
16. As though He had not heard them
17. They continued asking Him
18. He lifted up Himself
19. "He that is without sin among you, let him first cast a stone at her."
20. a. Stooped b. Wrote
21. a. Convicted b. Out
22. Beginning at the eldest even to the last
23. a. Jesus b. Woman
24. a. Lifted b. Saw
25. a. Accusers b. Condemned
26. "No man, Lord."
27. a. Condemn b. Sin
28. "I am the light of the world..."
29. a. Darkness b. Light
30. The Pharisees
31. a. Record b. Record
32. Yes
33. His record was true
34. a. Came b. Go
35. a. Came b. Go
36. After the flesh
37. He judged no man
38. It would have been true
39. Because He was not alone
40. The Father that sent Him
41. That the testimony of two men is true
42. a. Witness b. Father
43. "Where is your Father?"
44. "You all neither know me, nor my Father."
45. They should have known His Father also
46. In the treasury
47. He was teaching in the Temple
48. Lay hands upon Him
49. Because His hour was not yet come
50. a. Way b. Seek c. Die d. Come
51. "Will He kill Himself?"
52. Because He said, "Where I go, you all cannot come."
53. No
54. a. Beneath b. Above c. World d. World
55. That they would die in their sins
56. If they did not believe that Jesus was the Messiah (he), they would die in their sins
57. They will die in their sins
58. "Who are you?"
59. "Even the same that I said unto you from the beginning."
60. a. Say b. Judge
61. a. True b. Heard
62. That He spoke to them about the Father
63. a. Know b. Know
64. Because His Father taught Him to speak those things
65. He that sent Him
66. God the Father
67. No
68. Because He always did the things that pleased Him
69. Many believed on Him
70. To continue in His Word
71. a. Disciples b. Truth
72. The Truth makes them free
73. a. Abraham's b. Bondage
74. "You all will be made free."
75. They are the servants of sin
76. a. Servant b. Abides
77. They are free indeed
78. a. Abraham's b. Kill
79. Because His Word had no place in them
80. That which He had seen of His Father
81. That which they had seen of their father
82. Abraham
83. They would do the works of Abraham
84. They wanted to kill Him
85. Because He told them the truth

86. From God

87. No

88. No

89. Their father

90. a. Fornication b. Father

91. They would love Him

92. Proceeded b. Came

93. God sent Him

94. His speech

95. Because they would not hear His Word

96. The Devil

97. The lusts (desires) of their father

98. A murderer

99. He did not abide in the truth

100. Because there was not truth in him

101. He speaks of his own

102. a. Liar b. Father

103. Because He told them the truth

104. No

105. They did not believe Him

106. They hear God's words

107. They do not hear God's words

108. No

109. No

110. The Devil

111. a. Samaritan b. Devil

112. a. Devil b. Honor c. Dishonor d. Glory e. Seeks, Judges

113. They would never see death

114. That He had a devil

115. a. Abraham b. Prophets

116. That if a man kept His saying that he would never taste of death

117. a. Greater b. Greater c. Make

118. Yes

119. That they were dead

120. That if He honored Himself, His honor was nothing

121. His Father

122. Their God

123. Yes

124. They did not know Him

125. He knew Him

126. He would become a liar

127. a. Knew b. Kept

128. a. Rejoiced b. Saw c. Glad

129. In Heaven

130. a. Fifty b. Abraham

131. "Before Abraham was, I am."

132. They took up stones to cast at Him

133. a. Hid b. Temple

134. a. Midst b. Passed

(John 9:1-41)

1. He passed by

2. He saw a man which was blind

3. From his birth

4. "Master, who did sin?"

5. a. Man b. Parents

6. Because he was born blind

7. a. Sinned b. Sinned

8. That the works of God should be made manifest in him

9. Work the works of Him that sent Him

10. While it is day

11. The night

12. No man can work

13. Yes

14. The Light of the world

15. a. Spat b. Clay c. Anointed

16. a. Go b. Wash

17. Sent

18. a. Went b. Washed c. Seeing

19. "Is this not he that sat and begged?"

20. a. Neighbors b. Blind

21. "This is he."

22. "He is like him."

23. "I am he."

24. "How were your eyes opened?"

25. a. Jesus b. Anointed c. Wash d. Went e. Washed f. Received

26. "Where is He?"

27. "I do not know."

28. The Pharisees

29. The Sabbath

30. How he had received his sight

31. a. Clay b. Washed c. See

32. "This man is not of God."

33. Because they did not think Jesus kept the Sabbath

34. "How can a man that is a sinner do such miracles?"

35. A division

36. "What do you say of Him, that He has opened your eyes?"

37. "He is a prophet."

38. No

39. His parents

40. a. Blind b. See

41. a. Son b. Blind c. Sees d. Age e. Speak

42. They feared the Jews

43. They would be put out of the synagogue

44. "He is of age; ask him."

45. Confessing Christ

46. To call again the man that was blind

47. a. God b. Sinner

48. "Whether He be a sinner or no, I do not know."

49. "Whereas I was blind, now I see."

50. a. Did b. Open

51. a. Told b. Hear c. Hear d. Disciples

52. They reviled him

53. a. Disciple b. Disciples c. God d. Where

54. a. Marvelous b. Opened c. Sinners

55. a. Worshippers b. Will

56. That any man opened the eyes of one that was born blind

57. That if He were not of God that He could do nothing

58. a. Sins b. Teach

59. They cast him out

60. That they had cast him out

61. He found him

62. "Do you believe on the Son of God?"

63. "Who is He, Lord, that I might believe on Him?"

64. a. Seen b. Talks

65. "Lord, I believe."

66. He worshipped Jesus

67. For judgment

68. a. See b. Blind

69. The Pharisees

70. "Are we blind also?"

71. They would have no sin

72. Their sin would remain

73. No

74. That Jesus was the Son of God

(John 10:1-42)

1. He that does not enter through the door of the sheepfold, but climbs up some other way

2. The shepherd of the sheep

3. He opens the door

4. They hear his voice

5. a. Calls b. Leads

6. a. Before b. Follow

7. Because they know his voice

8. a. Follow b. Flee

9. Because they do not know the voice of strangers

10. A parable

11. No

12. The Door of the sheep

13. Thieves and robbers

14. The sheep did not hear them

15. The Door

16. a. Saved b. In, out c. Pasture

17. a. Steal b. Kill c. Destroy

18. a. Life b. Abundantly

19. The Good Shepherd

20. He would give His life for the sheep

21. a. Shepherd b. Sheep

22. a. Leaves b. Flees

23. a. Catches b. Scatters

24. a. Hireling b. Care

25. The Good Shepherd

26. a. Knows b. Known

27. The Father

28. The Father

29. Lay down His life for the sheep

30. Other sheep that were not of that fold

31. a. Bring b. Hear

32. One sheepfold

33. One shepherd

34. Because He laid down His life, that He might take it again

35. No man

36. Because He laid it down by Himself

37. a. Lay b. Take

38. The Father

39. He gave Himself for our sins

40. A division

41. a. Devil b. Mad c. Hear

42. "These are not the words of one that has a devil."

43. "Can a devil open the eyes of the blind?"

44. The Feast of the Dedication

45. Winter

46. Solomon's Porch

47. The Jews

48. "How long do you make us doubt?"

49. "If you are the Christ, tell us plainly."

50. a. Told b. Believe

51. The works that He did in His Father's name

52. Because they were not of His sheep

53. Yes

54. a. Hear b. Know c. Follow d. Give e. Perish
f. Pluck

55. a. Gave b. Greater

56. No man

57. They are one

58. No

59. No

60. No man

61. They took up stones to stone Him

62. Many good works

63. "For which of those works do you all stone me?"

64. a. Good b. Blasphemy c. God

65. Yes

66. "You all are gods."

67. The one unto whom the Word of God came

68. They cannot be broken

69. a. Sanctified b. Sent

70. "You blaspheme."

71. Because He said, "I am the Son of God."

72. If He did not do the works of His Father

73. They should believe the works

74. a. Know b. Believe

75. To take Him

76. He escaped out of their hand

77. Beyond Jordan

78. John the Baptist first baptized there

79. He abode (remained)

80. Many resorted to Him

81. a. Miracle b. True

82. Many believed on Him there

CPSIA information can be obtained
at www.ICGtesting.com
Printed in the USA
LVOW03s1431040416

482082LV00044B/1076/P